TAKING MY GOD FOR A WALK

"Tony's pilgrimage challenges on all levels — from aching feet and exhaustion to the deep longing within him to connect soul to soul with the God he loves. Whether you're about to don your walking boots or just to take an armchair pilgrimage of faith, this book will move and inspire you."

PAM RHODES, AUTHOR AND BROADCASTER

"Tony Collins' new book is an absolute delight. We take not one walk with him, but two, and both are a genuine pleasure. Here is a man who stands at the verge of retirement, who looks back and forward, and does so with both reverence and great good humour. There is so much quiet passion contained within these pages, and so many powerful lessons. Highly recommended."

DAVIS BUNN, BESTSELLING AUTHOR

"Engagingly insightful, endearingly witty, and wholly honest, this account of Tony's adventure will whet your appetite, as it has mine, to embark on your own pilgrimage into self-discovery and deeper richness of life."

SIMON GUILLEBAUD, AUTHOR AND MISSIONARY

"*Reading Tony Collins's tale of thirty-two days upon pilgrimage provides a reader with much of the experience of the journey, except for aching knees and blisters. Tony began the trek hoping to 'put myself in a situation where, if God were inclined to speak to me, I would be in a state of mind to listen'. It becomes apparent as the book ends that this did indeed happen. If one cannot make the pilgrimage to San Juan de Compostela, reading* Taking My God for a Walk *is an excellent substitute.*"

MEL STARR, AUTHOR OF *THE UNQUIET BONES*

"*A truly wonderful book: part travelogue, part history, part journal. Tony writes with wit, charm and intelligence, and above all, honesty. If, like me, you find yourself nodding in recognition with Tony's struggles with the busyness, clutter and 'stuff' of life that accumulates and drowns out space, clarity and God then the book will gently challenge you to reflect on your own priorities. We may not all be able to walk the Camino, but the lessons Tony learnt about life, himself and God, are ones we can all learn from. Tony's journey along the Camino left him changed – and I hope this beautifully written book may change you too. Now, where are my walking boots...*"

ANDY BANNISTER, EVANGELIST, SPEAKER AND
AUTHOR OF *THE ATHEIST WHO DIDN'T EXIST*

"*Veteran British publisher Tony Collins calls us to join him along the famous Camino pilgrimage path, guiding us through its beautiful, gritty, punishing terrain. Joy, pain, regret, discovery – you experience them all on a journey like this.*"

SHERIDAN VOYSEY, WRITER AND SPEAKER

"This is a pilgrimage on paper. The words are like the whisper of God on the evening breeze. The images painted are like glimpses of the dawn after a long night. Tony's pilgrimage is that of a man who is learning to fall upwards, in the words of Richard Rohr. You hear the depth of his faith and the yearning of a heart that knows God is so much bigger than any of our limited notions of Him and so much more beautiful than our most beautiful thoughts and ideas of Him.

"I found Tony's words deeply moving for a couple of reasons. Firstly, this is a walk I yearn to take for myself. I have dreamt of it for many years. Maybe one day, but for now I am grateful to Tony for helping me to feel the dirt of the Pyrenees beneath my feet and sense the scent of the air in my nostrils. His words have helped me walk, by proxy, a walk I will one day make for myself, God willing. Secondly, by the time you read these words, my sister, Anne, will have walked part of this pilgrimage for herself. She is making the journey as she comes to terms with the death of her son and husband to suicide between November 2014 and April 2015. I have already spoken some of Tony's words to her and they have been immensely powerful for her.

"Pilgrimage is something my particular strand of the Church does rather poorly and as a result we are impoverished. Tony's book is not just a record of his journey, it is a beautifully crafted, hope-laden invitation to us all to put on our walking boots, pack a small rucksack and embark on our own journey of discovering more of God and more of ourselves. I pray we each respond to the invitation and find ourselves with a fresh love of God and fresh awareness of our place and purpose in His world."

MALCOLM DUNCAN, AUTHOR, SPEAKER AND LEADER

TAKING MY GOD FOR A WALK

A publisher on pilgrimage

TONY COLLINS

MONARCH
BOOKS

Oxford UK, and Grand Rapids, USA

Published by Monarch Books
an imprint of
Lion Hudson plc
Wilkinson House, Jordan Hill Road,
Oxford OX2 8DR, England
Email: monarch@lionhudson.com
www.lionhudson.com/monarch

ISBN 978 0 85721 773 8
e-ISBN 978 0 85721 774 5

First edition 2016

Acknowledgments
Scripture quotations marked ESV are from The Holy Bible, English Standard Version® (ESV®) copyright © 2001 by Crossway, a publishing ministry of Good News Publishers. All rights reserved.
Scripture quotations marked NIV taken from the Holy Bible, New International Version Anglicised. Copyright © 1979, 1984, 2011 Biblica, formerly International Bible Society. Used by permission of Hodder & Stoughton Ltd, an Hachette UK company. All rights reserved. "NIV" is a registered trademark of Biblica. UK trademark number 1448790.
Scripture quotations marked NKJV taken from the New King James Version. Copyright © 1982 by Thomas Nelson, Inc. Used by permission. All rights reserved.

Illustrations by Lola Chapman

A catalogue record for this book is available from the British Library

Printed and bound in the UK, May 2016, LH26

For Ember, with my love

Contents

Acknowledgments

Several people have fingerprints on this book, notably Ali Hull, who badgered me unmercifully until I started writing it, and then offered valuable editorial input; Andrew Hodder-Williams, whose perceptive comments significantly tightened and sharpened the text; Jenny Ward and Jess Tinker, whose energy, enthusiasm, and intelligence have done so much to develop the Monarch and Lion Fiction lists, and who carried most of the load while I was gallivanting round Spain; Roger Chouler, book designer extraordinaire; Andrew Wormleighton, Simon Cox, Leisa Nugent, Rhoda Hardie, and Rob Wendover, my colleagues in sales and marketing, whose sane and pithy comments have kept me focused. Copy-editor Julie Frederick prevented some embarrassing blunders. Thank you all.

The Revd Douglas Wren put the thought in my mind. His example and advice were seminal.

Dr Mike Cooper shared his own photographic record and slightly hair-raising reminiscences of cycling the Camino – a particularly challenging enterprise – and lent me his copy of Tim Moore's *Spanish Steps*.

Thanks to Tim Moore, whom I have never met, but whose entertaining and improbable adventures with a donkey were my companion on the Way.

I owe my biggest debt however to Ember (Pen Wilcock), whose input and continuing encouragement, to undertake the pilgrimage, and then to write the book, have been of critical importance. Her company is an ongoing joy.

Foreword

Tony Collins has been my faithful friend and publisher for many years now. I have been truly blessed to know him both as a personal friend and as a professional aid to my writing projects. Even in his retirement, Tony has continued to assist me in my work as an author, which is so appreciated by me, as an author can only do so much without a good publisher! Tony is warm, generous, and hard-working. I have long admired him for these character traits, and I have long benefited from their use on my behalf. Tony is truly worthy of the highest admiration, and I am honoured to count him as a friend.

In *Taking My God for a Walk*, we encounter another side of Tony to the one often seen in his role as a publisher. Though I have long admired Tony for the qualities that I have mentioned above, I have not always seen in my interactions with him the same *adventurous* qualities that he reveals to the reader of this new book about his pilgrimage. Tony tells of the physical adventure that he takes in leaving his familiar world behind and plunging into the unknown on the Way of St James, but there is a different adventure in the spiritual side of his quest. Tony himself points out that it is the spiritual aspect of his journey that has the most lasting significance. He is embarking on an inward journey to understand himself and his place in relation to God. He seeks to hear God's word to him through the isolation of his pilgrimage.

Most of us experience the need at some point to take a step back and re-evaluate our place in life. *Taking My God for a Walk* comes as a refreshing chance to do this mentally, by going along with Tony Collins on his journey to understand God's relationship to him more profoundly, and thereby to come to a deeper understanding of himself. Tony invites us to become fellow pilgrims with him, and he shares with us some of the spiritual benefits of being a pilgrim. His conscience is now more tender. His understanding of himself is deeper. And, perhaps most important, he has opened himself to prayer and relationship with God in a new way. As someone who has experienced travel outside my country of birth for many years, I must confess that I feel like a pilgrim myself at times, and I can attest to the powerful ways God can work in the heart and soul of a wanderer who is open to Him. I am so pleased to recommend *Taking My God for a Walk* as a fine account of a pilgrimage, and as a fine way to take a mental pilgrimage oneself.

Canon Andrew White

- Boots, well broken in. Check.

- Walking poles, spring-loaded. Check.

- Pack, light blue, capacious. Check.

- Socks: several pairs, inner and outer. More of these anon. Check.

- Trousers and T shirts, underwear, fleece, cagoule. Check. Check.

- Medical kit, with plasters, paracetamol, Imodium, various prescription drugs, needles for blisters. No razor: I would join the ranks of the shaggy. Check.

- Loo roll. Knife. Torch. Hat, a faithful old friend. Tin mug. Check.

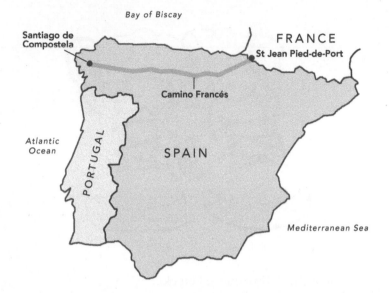

Prologue

This is the story of a long walk following the primary route of the Camino, the Way of St James, a path of devotion for pilgrims from across Europe for over a thousand years. To go on pilgrimage was an idea sown by a friend of mine, which had seized my imagination: it seemed profoundly right, a time apart, a chance to take stock.

It is also the story of three journeys.

At the simplest level, it is a journey of exploration across northern Spain. This outward journey, discovering landscapes and foods and people and customs, took place just a few hundred miles from my home, yet proved profoundly and occasionally shockingly alien.

It is also an historical journey, one which sent me delving into politics and demographics and religion, reading and researching and encountering twists of language and shards of architecture, endlessly fascinating, a series of fractals where each horizon gives way to the next.

In both these journeys I confess myself a novice, barely equipped to formulate the obvious questions, yet filled with glee at the discoveries which so many have made before me.

The third, the journey inwards, should have been familiar territory. I can be a solitary man, not above brooding, often buffeted by psychic weather. Yet the days on the Camino exposed me to dark days and whirlpools – and episodes of purest joy – which I had candidly failed to anticipate. I had gone seeking sources of reverence, but I had not imagined their impact.

All three journeys proved rewarding, but this last has stayed with me. It has convinced me of the enduring relevance of pilgrimage. If this account proves entertaining and profitable, then dust off your walking boots, prise open a space in your diary, and become a pilgrim too.

A Reason to Go
Day 1

My study was a tip, a trash heap, a familiar embarrassment. Most editors are pretty challenged in the desk department.

The evening before I left on pilgrimage I stared at the tottering stacks of dusty paper. Assuming I made it back, who would want to return to such a pit?

Over the previous days I had organized, tied up ends, briefed my very able colleagues, fretted over travel plans, weighed and discarded and packed. I was stressed, and so weary: tired to the bone.

Contemplating the overflowing bin, I reflected ruefully that the media world is about creating impressions. At least part of my job is making people look good. I had worked to the very last minute, obsessively firing off emails and trying to second-guess the future. But why should my family, who live with the unpolished original, tolerate my mess?

In my eyrie under the roof of our elderly-but-serviceable Edwardian house, at the top of a hill in an English coastal town, I herded paper into black bin liners. I believe deeply in simplicity, but it requires vigilance. Disposing of crud should be a daily discipline, but I had lost the habit.

As I cleaned house it came to me that this was truly the start of my journey.

Publishing is an absorbing game of chance, punctuated by elation and dismay. The margins are tiny and the salaries modest, but you meet unusual people and sometimes books change lives. At its best the ideas matter profoundly and the words fizz with passion and beauty.

It's a dubious trade, however. In choosing suitable words you come to distrust them, and those who use them too freely. Rightly so. An unimpressed acquaintance once described me as "so smooth he could slide up a hill". I have long feared that Jane Austen's choice for my namesake, her unctuous vicar, was not a matter of chance.

On pilgrimage, sliding up a hill could prove useful.

Hastings station at dawn was bleak and chilly, dotted with silent travellers, policed by silent seagulls. Pen kissed me goodbye. I waved to her, took a seat, pulled out my notebook, and stopped short. How do you describe a plunge into the unknown?

In the dark window I saw an ageing, white-haired geezer, eyes prickling as the train gathered speed. I was suddenly sad, and slightly terrified.

This was not the first time I had stepped over the edge.

Decades previously I had trained as a missionary. A meeting with an American based in Brazil had changed my trajectory entirely. The director of Christian World Publishing in São

Paulo, he was looking for a Christian with linguistic training and experience in the world of books.

My first wife Jane and I were French graduates, so the prospect of learning another language was fun rather than daunting. For several years I had worked for Hodder & Stoughton, by that point heading their religious editorial section. It was a good job, and worth doing. But the office politics of the period got to me, and my innards were playing up.

We were deeply involved in our church – St Nicholas, Sevenoaks – where we ran the Young Adults group, taught teenagers, attended a house group, and had a hand in various dramatic endeavours. I had explored a call to the ordained ministry, but my parish priest objected to my enthusiasm for the then-novel charismatic movement (which fascinated me, and still does) and refused to endorse my candidacy.

Jane and I were not sure what to do. Our first daughter, Abigail, had just been born. I was no longer young, in indifferent health, and starting to detest my job.

Then we met an American, Peter Cunliffe, who is something of a legend in the world of Christian books. A quietly spoken, deeply committed man, Peter is a lover of the Scriptures, for whom the task of getting out the Word goes hand in glove with good accounting practice: a sound, wise publisher. Peter was seeking someone, a linguist and Christian publisher, to replace him in São Paulo, so that he could – in his fifties – start studying French, with the intention of rescuing an ailing Parisian publisher, Editions Farel.

It sounded a fine thing, to be a missionary. Could I step into his shoes? With youthful chutzpah, I thought I might.

However, there was a snag: no salary.

Disembarking among the frowsty commuters at Victoria station, I hoisted my brand new rucksack to my shoulders. On the Tube I had to unship it again and straddled the bulky thing, taking up far too much space and generating unfriendly glances.

The Stansted Express from Liverpool Street stood blissfully empty, and with a rising pulse I installed my baggage in a corner: the unfamiliar swanky train, functional and smart, represented *terra incognita*.

In the late 1970s the idea of raising your own support was alien to British minds, though well established in the States.

Since her teens Jane had been convinced she would be a missionary in South America. We decided to talk to the South American Missionary Society, whose headquarters were a few miles away in Tunbridge Wells. Would they second us to work with Peter?

One interview followed another. We enjoyed linguistic tests, and completed devastating application forms. One page was blank apart from a line at the top: "What do you consider to be your major personality defects?" If necessary, take more paper, I added mentally.

Another question caused more trouble: "What do you most enjoy?" A commercial animal, I responded, "Selling things." My interviewers, good missionaries all, were scandalized. I couldn't see the problem. Cars, books, Jesus. I was a callow youth.

In due course we were asked back to hear whether SAMS would sponsor us. "We believe you are truly called," the General Secretary told my wife. He paused, and turned to face me squarely. "We are not sure about you."

They laid down a challenge. "You may know a bit about publishing," they told me, "but you don't have a clue about mission. Go and get trained, and we'll consider you. Apply to All Nations."(All Nations Christian College, in Ware, Hertfordshire, remains a leading provider of mission training.)

Two nail-biting interviews later we received the much-hoped for news that All Nations had places for us.

On that slender semi-promise from SAMS we put our house on the market. I handed in my notice. Our church agreed to pray for us and contribute to our costs. We told our friends. Jane's mother started researching air fares to Brazil. Our picture appeared in a local paper. Our second daughter, Carrie, arrived late but safely.

With a sense of burning boats we headed north to Ware.

In the intervening years I had made other big decisions, and some grisly mistakes. None felt so large, or promised so much instant disaster, as the challenge of the Way.

At Spring Harvest[1] that year, the year of pilgrimage, I had met Douglas, an old acquaintance, a cleric from a village near Tunbridge Wells. I was swiftly struck by a change in my friend – a crispness, a new confidence, a willingness to take the lead. Over beer I asked what had happened.

"I went on the Camino," he replied, as if that explained all. "Best thing I've ever done."

The Camino de Santiago is the route, or rather routes, followed by pilgrims over the last thousand years to the shrine of St James in north-west Spain. Celebrated in the 2010 film *The Way*, the Camino has become steadily more popular since the 1990s: over 215,000 pilgrims walked a sufficient length of the Way in the course of 2013 to gain their *compostelas*, their certificates of pilgrimage.

---

1 One of the UK's larger Christian festivals.

Of these by far the largest number followed the Camino Frances, the French Way. It is a very long walk. The Camino Frances runs across the French border first south then west, through Pamplona, Burgos, and Leon before climbing into Galicia. By the time you have reached Santiago you will have covered 490 miles, or slightly more than the distance between Hastings, my home town, and Edinburgh.

I had a sabbatical long overdue, courtesy of my generous employers. I had pondered a kind of world tour, lecturing, visiting authors and publishers, being quietly significant. Some spark of honesty informed me this was narcissistic tosh. I was troublingly aware that I tended to stay where it was safe and I knew what I was doing. By that point I was a senior member of a respected publishing company and a Reader in the Church of England – solid positions, with a faint whiff of prestige.

I had taken some fairly hairy risks in the course of my life, but now, month by month, my life was trundling along in respectable grooves. My children were grown. My first marriage had finally fallen apart, after thirty years: a distressing period, but I was now most happily hitched to a very talented writer and long-term friend. My stepdaughters made me welcome. I was content, solvent, comfortable.

Something niggled. Too much comfort clogs the arteries. Like the paper on my desk, it accumulates. Time, I felt, to clean the stables; to take stock; to ream out, to decoke. To take risks, to cross boundaries.

The Camino seemed ideal. I don't speak Spanish. I had no idea whether my creaking bones could cope. The Way is dotted with *albergues* – hostels – but they don't usually accept reservations, so each day I would set out not knowing where, or whether, a bed would await me. I would spend day after day alone. I might break something, or fall off something. Something might fall off me. I would probably get lost. I would certainly get tired, cold, hungry, and wet.

Pen thought it a great idea, and held me to my plans when the doubts mounted.

I wanted to be a pilgrim, not a tourist, not a reporter. Jesus' injunction to his disciples in Luke 9 rang in my mind: "Take nothing for the journey – no staff, no bag, no bread, no money, no extra shirt." I failed on precisely every single detail. However, I packed neither tablet nor camera. I left my smartphone on my desk and bought a basic mobile. A Moleskine notebook and cheap biro completed the communications package.

This was not a deprivation. I had grown leery of social media: too intrusive, too shouty. (My director, in a felicitous phrase, once compared Twitter to standing in front of a fire hose. Exactly.) I had had my fill of conversation. A refugee from a profession much given to networking, I hungered after isolation.

Would I, on my return, feel sufficiently integrated to activate my Facebook account?[2]

I was also a refugee from stuff.

When we arrive on Planet Earth we may be trailing clouds of glory, but soon we are trailing junk. Like cholesterol deposits, the heirlooms and mementos accumulate. *I couldn't possibly get rid of that; it was my grandmother's.* You move house transferring boxes from one attic to the next. My wife is fond

---

2   See p. 243

of quoting Toinette Lippe:[3] "Problems arise when things accumulate."

Over the previous years we had done our best to dispose of clutter. Our home has few ornaments. Pen, the leader in this enterprise, has her possessions down to a couple of boxes and a short clothes rack. I still cherish a few hundred books, but have cleared many thousands through Oxfam. The regular collection bags from The Salvation Army, soliciting clothes, rarely go unregarded.

When my parents died I found boxes of photo albums in their attic, full of faces without names, places without locations, images of forgotten holidays and long-extinct friends. Most went back to the interwar years, and found their way swiftly to the bin. Over the years I have been the primary chronicler of my own family, the man behind the shutter. With focus and a steady hand I have weeded out the dross, but there are still a couple of hundred choice images, which, along with the best of the heirlooms, I have handed on to my younger daughter. She has my permission not to do the same to her sons.

I subscribe to a creed that claims to value a man for who he is, not for what he owns. A pilgrim should carry very little, or he won't get far.

But there is more than one kind of accretion. Like Bunyan's hero I was toting baggage, much of it distressingly acquired since my conversion to the Christian faith in my late teens: fears, resentments, insecurities, ambitions, defences.

---

3 Another editor: indeed, an editor's editor. The very erudite Ms Lippe was for many years rights director and senior editor at Knopf, and is author of *Nothing Left Over: A Plain and Simple Life*, New York: Tarcher/Putnam, 2002.

This seemed an ideal opportunity to jettison mental detritus, truly to clean house.

There is another reason for going on pilgrimage, of course. When you apply at Santiago Cathedral for your certificate of pilgrimage, your *compostela*, they inspect your *credencial* – your pilgrim passport, your stamped record of places visited – and ask if you have been travelling for reasons of religion, spirituality or tourism.

In the great era of European pilgrimage – roughly speaking, from the eleventh to the fourteenth century – pilgrims travelled for reasons that could be broadly classified as religious: to do penance, to seek remission of sins, to receive healing, to make more immediate contact with the Almighty, or at least evidence of the presence of one of His saints, in the form of a holy relic. In a world without set holidays, where most stayed within their manor, pilgrimage offered an adventure for the restless. It was also a genuine challenge: the Way is dotted with pilgrim cemeteries, and of a certainty with thousands of unmarked graves. To be a pilgrim, and to return, was no mean feat.

So what of modern pilgrims? Of those to whom I put the question as we walked, or over a glass of wine, a few were active Christians, allowing space for the divine. More sought a spiritual connection, undefined. Some were there for the excursion, or to plunge into history. "Just havin' fun," observed Mack, a US Marine.[4]

Did I have a spiritual motive? I have been a Christian

---

4 There are no such creatures as ex-Marines, as Mack later pointed out. There are Marines no longer on active service, but in this respect Marines and bishops are as one: the title endures. Semper Fi.

much of my life, mostly in the evangelical strand of the faith. However, prayer and worship have always posed a challenge. My moments of revelation have been infrequent, and partial. A buzzing fly inside me is always seeking the next task, the next distraction, the next set of data. I surf on stress. I am not great at contemplation, church is too often a bore, and songs of praise a struggle. My prayer life feels real, but it stutters.

This has always bothered me, that I should prefer paperwork to worship. But I am in excellent company. In his *Pensées* the mathematician and mystic Blaise Pascal wrote, "Distraction is the only thing that consoles us, and yet it is itself the greatest of our miseries." Peter Kreeft, in his *Christianity for Modern Pagans*, comments on Pascal's teaching:

> We want to complexify our lives. We don't have to, we want to. We want to be harried and hassled and busy. Unconsciously, we want the very things we complain about. For if we had leisure, we would look at ourselves and listen to our hearts and see the great gaping hole in our hearts and be terrified, because that hole is so big that nothing but God can fill it.[5]

Douglas Adams offers a related point in his description of the "Total Perspective Vortex", the most horrible means of torture to which a sentient being can be subjected, in *The Restaurant at the End of the Universe*:

> When you are put into the Vortex you are given just one momentary glimpse of the entire unimaginable

---

5 San Francisco: Ignatius Press, 1993.

> infinity of creation, and somewhere in it a tiny little
> mark, a microscopic dot on a microscopic dot, which
> says, "You are here."[6]

Ever since I had read the Christian Pascal, and a few years later the atheist Adams, I had been aware that sooner or later I would have to face the vacuum for myself.

This was uncomfortable territory. As a publisher of Christian books I have never required my authors to agree with me, or I with them. The role of editor, like that of journalist, is to comment and assess, not to participate. It is necessary, for the job to be well done, that you maintain a measure of objectivity. A good editor is self-effacing, serving his or her authors: the task is to assist, to challenge, to be a wise friend.

To a degree you become a Vicar of Bray, a chameleon. I trained at Hodder under that doyen of the publishing world, Edward England, an elegant but stalwart evangelical with a Salvation Army background. When he was editing the autobiography of Cardinal Heenan, the leader of Britain's Catholics, in the early 1970s, the respect was warm and mutual. Much later the Cardinal's staff were discomfited to learn that their boss's editor might have been a man of faith, but a Catholic he was not.

The problem is not just that of blending smoothly into every foreground. It is easy to get fired up by a book or an author, and every writer needs an advocate in house, or their book will be cast adrift, contract or no. This is one part of the editor's task: to sell the book to your sceptical colleagues, and to go on sponsoring as necessary. No-holds-barred

---

6 London: Pan Books, 1980.

endorsement creates expensive mistakes, however, and so you need to stand slightly to one side as the juggernaut of conviction rumbles by. You become adept at easy enthusiasm.

But there is a cost, familiar to editors and journalists alike: the layby is an austere environment, where rubbish accumulates and weeds grow.

As I would discover, the Camino is in some respects a blank page. You walk, and you think. Possibly you pray. Distractions are minimized. The Vortex is your steady companion. I wanted to put myself in a situation where, if God were inclined to speak to me, I would be in a state of mind to hear.

And so, alongside my Moleskine and my rinky-dinky mobile, I took my Kindle, loaded – along with Tim Moore's excellent *Spanish Steps*[7] (his entertaining account of walking the Camino with a donkey) – with a Bible, and Pen's book of Lenten readings, *The Wilderness Within You*.[8]

I had played the critic too long. It was time to join the cast.

---

7   London: Jonathan Cape, 2004.

8   Penelope Wilcock, *The Wilderness Within You*, Oxford: Monarch Books, 2013.

St Jean Pied-de-Port
Days 1 and 2

One of the main starting points for the Camino Frances is a mountain village on the French/ Spanish border, St Jean Pied-de-Port. Fly from Stansted to Biarritz, then catch the stopping train.

Stansted Airport, shiny and efficient, is a slightly unreal departure point for a journey to the medieval world. In the queue for Ryanair's services I looked over my companions, trying to spot someone on a similar quest, notable for his noble mien, his gaze fixed on infinity. Or her eminently sensible boots.

My curiosity had a purpose. The guidebook suggested an alternative to the slow and infrequent train: a taxi straight to St Jean, economical if shared. No joy. The aircraft seemed packed with sun worshippers in search of their fix.

Standing in the autumn warmth on the Biarritz tarmac I finally spotted a fellow pilgrim, instantly recognizable by his hat and backpack. I approached, hoping to share dreams, information, and a cab.

"Nope, just going home," he responded. An entirely

British raspberry farmer with the unlikely name of Jean-Paul, he lived outside Biarritz. "But I've walked bits of the Camino," he volunteered. "You see some crazy people. I met one guy pushing a shopping trolley."

Jean-Paul was headed for the local railway station, a few miles by bus, and helpfully guided me to the right stop. As we swung through down-at-heel French suburbs I pressed him for advice. He thought. "Look up," he offered finally. "People spend their entire journey staring at their feet. If you look up you may spot a stork. Or a vulture."

An elegant bar dominated the station concourse. A lissom young waitress served me a lager and a *sandwich au jambon*.

Unmistakeable pilgrims, silent and pensive, occupied adjoining tables. I proffered the taxi idea, but no nibbles. "We *want* to take the slow train," observed an Austrian girl, fluently but tartly. "It is beautiful."

I realized uneasily that I was still on a schedule. Recognizing a small turning point sidling up, I stared at my wrist. An inveterate last-minute merchant, for years I had kept every timepiece fifteen minutes fast, all part of the security blanket. With a sense of occasion I removed my watch to correct it, and checked the station clock. By French time I was forty-five minutes slow. I could have missed my train.

As I sat there my mobile pinged. Pen had texted an Irish blessing.

> May the long time sun shine upon you,
> all love surround you,
> and the pure light within you carry you all the way home.

"Praying for you every day," she added. "I have you in my heart."

On the platform at Biarritz station I joined a cheerful group. Michael, a fit young German cameraman, had walked the Camino that spring, and was now doing it all over again to make a documentary. I looked at him with increased respect, and he grinned.

"There are four stages to a pilgrimage," he told me. "The body, the mind, the stage of love, and the stage of parting."

The little local train finally chugged into the station, and departed again crammed with pilgrims. As we clanked up through the chestnut-wooded foothills of the Pyrenees, crossing and re-crossing an ever-faster mountain stream, I stared in disquiet at the increasingly vertical scenery and wondered if I would ever make it beyond stage one.

I enjoy entertaining French nationals with my version of their language. But while we plugged away at the gradient, pausing briefly in every tiny halt, I realized that though I had been expecting the transition to Spanish, I was unprepared for Basque. As I tried to get my tongue around one impossibly unpronounceable set of consonants after another, and saw emblazoned on every rock and wall the Basque colours of white over red, it came to me that "Spain" might be a name on a map, but to quite a lot of people on that map it does not describe their homeland. Spain is an archipelago.

Before leaving home I had registered myself with the London-based Confraternity of St James,[9] and received their rather lurid mustard-yellow Pilgrim's Record, whose

---

9 The Confraternity is a UK-based charity established to promote the pilgrimage to the shrine of St James in Santiago de Compostela. It provides information to assist prospective pilgrims, of all religions or none, who are planning a journey along one of the many routes to Santiago. If you are minded to try the Camino for yourself, start here.

blank pages would serve as my *credencial*. With it came their regular "Bulletin", a slightly alarming amalgam of stories, slivers of history, memories, and reports which all carried, to my editor's nostrils, a scent of deepest conviction, and left me slightly nervous: in this company, was I a flake? In the enthusiastic world of the Confraternity, it seemed, you could not dabble. But what did it take to become a real pilgrim?

St Jean Pied-de-Port – St John's at the Foot of the Pass – exists to serve the pilgrim trade, each ancient house on the winding central street offering budget accommodation or your choice of authentic pilgrim's staff. St Jean forms the last stop on the French side of the border for pilgrims coming from Paris, Vézelay or Le Puy before the tough mountain crossing. As I afterwards discovered, the original town (Saint-Jean-le-Vieux) was obliterated by Richard the Lionheart in 1177: tactless, to say the least, and easily misunderstood, but today the British euro seemed welcome.

At the modest station we alighted en masse into the setting sun, stretching and muttering. The train emptied completely: this was the end of the line.

I wrestled my pack onto my shoulders and followed the stream of travellers up the steep road, through the gate in the high defensive walls,[10] and into the core of the town, stumbling over the cobbled streets and admiring the ancient houses of pink and grey stone, old when the Revolution came. I eventually located the Pilgrim Centre. It was after eight o'clock – I had missed the Monday market, when sheep and cattle are driven into the little town – but the centre was still crowded, with practical ladies ranged behind tables.

---

10 Rebuilt by the kings of Navarre after they were certain Richard had quit the area.

I waited in line, and proffered my *credencial*. My interviewer examined this curiously: the first such response of many. It later became clear that while the Confraternity (a British institution) is well established, Brits are comparatively rare beasts on the Way, accounting for less than 2 per cent of the whole.[11] Fewer still are members of the Confraternity. My all-too-visible booklet would provoke comment all the way to Santiago.

I dutifully received some instructions, a sheet of emergency numbers, warnings about bad weather, and my first *sello* or stamp, with a green representation of a medieval traveller.

Every hostel and bar has its own stamp: it is possible to collect hundreds, each one different and some a little jolt of beauty. These are an indispensable part of the Camino, and enable you to demonstrate that you have visited the locations you claim (though they are helpfully silent should the flagging pilgrim opt for a taxi). The *credencial* is your passport to an inexpensive, dry, safe lodging: it shows you are playing the game. Most *credencials* are not my gaudy affair, but simple cards, folded concertina-wise, and by journey's end dappled with overlapping *sellos*, a memento no shop can supply, and ideal for framing.

It will not spoil your enjoyment of the film *The Way*[12] if I explain that it starts with a death: a young man is caught in a violent storm as he crosses the Pyrenees, and perishes. The

---

11 Statistics provided by the pilgrim office in Santiago.

12 Directed by Emilio Estevez and released in 2010. Martin Sheen plays an ophthalmologist who walks the Way in memory of his son. A fine film, and excellent preparation.

path over the pass, as I discovered the following day, is marked by snow posts, and near the peak, shortly before the Spanish border, stands a mountain hut for the use of travellers.

However, there are two options. In bad weather, or if you are inexperienced, John Brierley[13] counsels, take the easier but less scenic and more populated Valcarlos route, which stays closer to the main road. The name Valcarlos derives from the emperor Charlemagne, who chose that route in the eighth century during his campaigns against the Moors.

Chicken to the core, I decided Charlemagne probably knew his stuff.

That first night, in the single hostel I had booked, two Portuguese cyclists, both fluent in English, invited me to share their meal. It was a hint of frequent generosity to come. Cyclists have a hard time on the Camino, they informed me rather wryly over pasta and beans: walkers think they are cheating. However, the namby-pamby Valcarlos option was not for my friends: they were headed for the obviously more noble Route Napoléon, so called because the great Bonaparte preferred it as a means of getting his troops in and out of Spain during the Peninsular War. Brierley adds that medieval pilgrims also chose this higher option because it avoided the bandits who haunted the tree-lined lower route. There are spectacular views, he observes helpfully, and fewer cars. The Route Napoléon reaches 1,450 metres, one of the highest points on the journey, and incidentally higher than the peak of Ben Nevis. The first stage covers 15 miles.

So: more ups, followed by precipitant downs, less shade, and lots of rocks. What was wrong with this picture?

---

13 Brierley's *A Pilgrim's Guide to the Camino de Santiago* is ubiquitous on the Way, regularly updated, and generally referred to as the Bible.

In the battle of the emperors, serious pilgrims evidently followed Napoleon. I sighed inwardly.

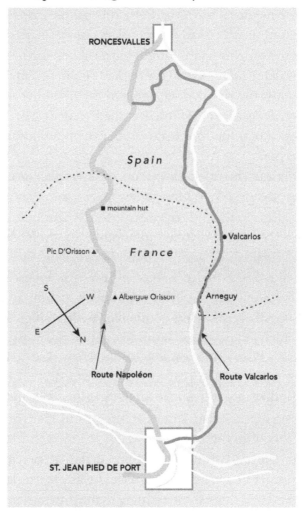

Breakfast was hot and fragrant French bread, fetched fresh from the bakery by our cheerful host, struggling up his narrow stairs with a vast armful of golden loaves.

I headed downhill into the grey dawn, in the wake of a trickle of other pilgrims. At the far end of the main street stands the medieval arch, the Porte d'Espagne, massive and uncompromising, that ushers travellers onto their journey. I unlimbered my shiny, new, bright blue, rubber-shod, spring-loaded walking poles, settled my pack, straightened my socks, strode across the river bridge, ignored the tempting signs to Valcarlos, and started to climb over the Pyrenees. My cycling friends sped past me, and I stared after them resentfully as I began to puff.

For those who look down on cycling pilgrims, such opinions are drivel. Within a few paces the Way leaves the metalled road and zigzags upwards through gorse, rock, and gravel. Anyone attempting to cycle such a route is certifiable, and a hero. In subsequent days I would encounter many bands of cyclists, focused and determined, but the one who comes most readily to mind was a supremely muscled gentleman with a single-wheel trailer which followed him lamb-like across the most rutted landscape. Time after time I would edge past a cyclist grunting with every step as he[14] slowly wheeled his mount upwards, then stand aside as he freewheeled crazily down the subsequent decline, stones spitting from his tyres, and disappeared into the haze.

Eheu, the path was steep. Spectacular = precipitous. Sweat began to course down my face. I was once a distance runner, and had done some training in the previous months, striding too confidently across the gentle undulations of Sussex, but nothing like enough. I stopped to gasp, stopped

---

14 Usually he. There are many female pilgrims, but few cycle, to my observation.

again to drink from the dangling tube of my camelback, stopped again to admire the intricately folded mountain scenery. Behind me straggled a line of red-faced pilgrims bent beneath bulky packs. Ahead, a series of khaki-clad bottoms ascended. It was not yet 9.00 a.m.

The path twisted left, disappearing between grey-brown outcrops of rock and thorn. The sun rose higher, and the air began to taste of thyme. My pack – pared to simplicity, but still worryingly heavy – set off a rictus beneath my left shoulder blade that would prove my companion for the next five weeks. My breath grew steadily more laboured and the pain in my chest intensified: particularly unwelcome, in the light of a brush with heart disease years previously. I hauled myself upwards with my walking poles, sometimes letting them dangle from my wrists as I heaved my unwilling carcase over boulders, grasping at tough shrubs and wincing as their rough bark lacerated my palms. The tiny track, inches wide, snaked between spiny bushes and crags.

Up, and further up. An hour or so into the day I passed the Auberge d'Orisson, perched on the mountain's flank. Cheerful garrulous pilgrims filled the benches outside and I joined them briefly on the rough wooden planks to down a bottle of water, glorious and achingly cold. Priority to people arriving on foot, says the auberge's website: so I should think.

Brierley describes the first stage, from St Jean on the French side to Roncesvalles on the Spanish, as "arduous but rewarding". Such enthusiasm. Shaking sweat from my eyes and cursing his remotest ancestors,[15] I craned my head back to try and spot the summit, and saw my first vulture.

---

15 Scoutmasters, the lot of them.

Griffon vultures are not cuddly. With a wing span of up to 2.5 metres, they tidy up the sheep pastured in the high mountain meadows. In the Pyrenees they are a common sight, with a population of at least 1,800 pairs, the largest concentration in the world. It was easy to imagine that they might fancy a more varied diet.

The Way, in fact, is genuinely slightly dangerous – less so than in the Middle Ages, when bandits preyed upon the pilgrim herds – but right along its length, all the way to Santiago, it is dotted with shrines, many recent, remembering those who have fallen. *The Way* is quite accurate: stray from the path here and you are at instant risk. More generally, deaths from heart attack, heat exhaustion, extreme weather, road traffic, all take their toll. Injuries are common, especially going downhill: on ensuing days I would meet many folk limping along with ghastly wince-making blisters, shin splints, twisted knees. Brierley drily advises, "The hospitals of Logroño, only 160 km away, specialize in treating foot and leg injuries sustained by over-eager pilgrims."

As if the vertical landscape were not challenge enough, I overhauled one swarthy young man with a ponytail who was making his cautious way upwards, only to discover that he was walking barefoot. We passed and repassed each other several times as one or another stopped to pant, and I finally left him behind when he sat down to rub Vaseline into his soles.

Every twist in the track brought a steeper slope: sometimes it was almost impossible to stand. My impossible pack grew impossibly heavier. The rocky footing demanded my full attention – I could hear Jean-Paul urging, "Look up!" I found myself pausing more and more frequently to appreciate Brierley's spectacular views, and by the time, hours later,

I finally clambered to the summit on marshmallow legs, winded and appalled, my self-confidence had been badly dented.

I was not sure I could do this. What had I taken on?

Confidence is a useful tool, but it can turn in your hand. So can faith, as I had discovered.

Jane and I had gone off to All Nations excited, and to a degree nervous. The studies were enthralling, and we quickly found our feet. Our fellow students were an impressive bunch, with thirty-two different nationalities represented in the 180-strong student body. There were surgeons, nurses, midwives, linguists, pastors, mechanics, business people, theologians, administrators. The college had a minimum age of twenty-five, and we found ourselves among a variety of young professionals expecting to be posted across the globe. Missionaries, like priests, do not deserve the amusement, pity, and condescension with which they are often treated, and our fellows would be heading out to assume awesome responsibilities.

The course was profoundly hands-on. A young Scottish friend of ours had recently qualified as a surgeon. His destination was a mission hospital in rural Tanzania, where he could be expected to perform emergency operations by the light of an ancient diesel generator, which regularly failed at the worst of moments. The college not only found him a model of the same generator, but also recruited a technician to train him in how to repair it in the dark – while, presumably, the patient slowly and distressingly regained consciousness.

I loved the practical stuff. At school I had been one of life's duffers when it came to anything practical: my first effort at carpentry was held up by the teacher as an example to avoid, and my metalwork was a source of mirth to my classmates. But by dint of rabid enthusiasm I had learned to tinker effectively with cars, and now I revelled in the weekly trips to a local technical college where a bemused lecturer assisted his slightly senior students to fix their collection of equally senior bangers.

I also discovered theology, and relished my fumbling encounters with New Testament Greek. The course included a brave attempt to teach us the rudiments of psychology, and this too I lapped up. What other course, anywhere, would include an introduction to transactional analysis before coffee, a seminar on Paul's approach to mission before lunch, and a demonstration of the best way to change a pair of brake shoes in the afternoon?

We met other young married couples on campus (some had fallen in love at college: romances were common). Husbands were expected to attend illustrated lectures on emergency midwifery. Our second daughter had been born in the weeks before term started, and I had attended the births of both girls, so I was less discountenanced than some of my green-hued colleagues.

A couple of health matters marred the two years at All Nations. We had hoped to have more children, but a drug I was taking rendered me infertile. This was an ongoing sadness, but we accepted it. We had two daughters, whom we loved dearly. It was enough.

More worryingly, at the end of the first year I felt too ill to get out of bed one morning. By the third day I was photophobic, and Jane called the doctor. He had no hesitation in diagnosing meningitis, and within half an hour two burly ambulance men were manoeuvring a stretcher down our narrow stairs. For the first forty-eight hours I was out of it, then came round to find my parents at the end of my hospital bed: for them, as for Jane's parents (who came hotfoot up from Cornwall), the disease brought memories of death.

The treatment worked swiftly, however, and I was released after a week. Jane's mother stayed on for a few days to help with the girls, then fell ill in turn – also, and most bizarrely, meningitis: bizarrely, because I had come down with the bacterial form and she had contracted the viral form, which she could not have caught from me. Jane's father turned the car around and drove back up from Cornwall, sitting for hours beside her in the same ward I had recently vacated. I think it was the first time in years they had truly talked, and afterwards their tempestuous marriage took a turn for the better.

Both she and I would make a full recovery, but there were unexpected consequences. The first was that both of us suffered, weeks later, from an attack of the blackest depression. For my mother-in-law, a mercurial lady, depression was part of her world, but to me it was a new experience, and instructive. I would later discover that depression is a common sequel to meningitis.

The second consequence was that the next time I attempted to give blood – up to that point a regular practice – I was politely, firmly, and forever turned away, my card marked, my vital fluids tainted. I was, to my amusement, a toxic brand.

It proved an eventful summer, not least because that July Hodder published *Prisoner Rejoice* by Nicole Valéry, which Jane and I had translated from the French at the behest of Romanian pastor Richard Wurmbrand[16] (Nicole had

---

16 Richard Wurmbrand, who wrote *Tortured for Christ*, had been imprisoned in the severest conditions (including three years in solitary confinement). He was one of the most articulate Christian critics of Marxist repression, and for many years became an emblem of courage for Western believers.

been imprisoned in a Romanian labour camp with Sabina Wurmbrand, Richard's wife). Simultaneously Hodder released a book Jane had written: *His God, My God*, which she had ghosted for Caroline Urquhart, the wife of the charismatic Christian leader Colin Urquhart. *Prisoner Rejoice* started well, but did not reprint; *His God, My God* performed superbly. The following year Hodder published a book I had ghosted for George Verwer,[17] *No Turning Back*. George's extraordinary ministry ensured that it sold and sold, to date in over thirty languages: it is still in print.

That summer, we made our farewells. It was time for us to move on. We had both become confident in Bible teaching and had learned how to preach a respectable sermon. We had made friends, established a routine of personal prayer, and kind but shrewd tutors had probed our vulnerabilities. The mission field will find the holes in your soul, they pointed out. Those of us who did not already have a job waiting had found a placement (there is little unemployment amongst missionaries).

We had a goal in view, we had relished our studies, and the South American Missionary Society had been true to its word: they were prepared to second us to work with Peter Cunliffe, with whom we had stayed in close contact. We spoke at churches, articulating our plans, and congregations and individuals promised to pray for us. We valued these commitments highly. Our course had sensitized us to the spiritual world, and anyone on the spiritual front line needs prayer support. It was time to start learning Portuguese.

His organization Voice of the Martyrs continues to aid Christians around the world who face persecution for their faith.

17   George Verwer, veteran missionary and visionary, is the founder of Operation Mobilisation, one of the world's largest mission agencies.

At this point our airship began to deflate. Our elder daughter Abigail was nearly four, and she had yet to learn to speak. She had been slow to stand and walk, slow to master potty training, and as we watched her younger sister's eager progress we grew increasingly aware our beautiful little girl was not developing properly.

Over the summer after we left All Nations a series of consultations ensued with child development experts. No one was prepared to put a name to Abbie's condition, but a consensus gradually emerged. Finally the day came we had been dreading. "If you take your daughter out of an English-language environment," the consultant told us, "the chances are she may never learn to speak."

It was a bleak moment. We returned home horrified and stunned. I alternated between rage and dismay. What was God playing at? We had been so sure we were following His instructions. Door after door had opened. There was a job to be done, and we were up for it. Had we misunderstood? Worse: was the whole edifice, the whole spiritual construct, a pack of cards? Above all, what was the future for Abbie?

We talked to our parents, our friends, our home church. With unforgettable generosity, our daughter's godmother, herself the mother of four, offered to take Abbie and raise her as her own child, so we could obey our commission and fulfil our dreams. At this point we realized we could not do it: our daughter came before our plans, and we would have to seek an accommodation with the Almighty.

Our confidence in ourselves, and in our faith, had been badly dented.

I passed the tiny mountain hut, constructed to provide shelter for pilgrims trapped by a change in the weather. Negotiating a cattle grid – the exact point, extraordinarily prosaic, where France becomes Spain – I stood for a moment at the summit to breathe, gather my wits, take a drink, and resettle my pack. With utterly misplaced relief I crossed the tarmacked road that follows the narrow ridge.

Now the impossible became worse, because the path abruptly deteriorated into precipitous scree.

Down is harder than up, as any runner knows, and in the course of that afternoon one girl broke her ankle on the descent. I found myself lurching from sliding rock to flimsy sapling. The French side of the Pyrenees is coated in scrub, dry and harsh; on the Spanish side the slopes are thickly wooded, home to one of the largest remaining beech forests in Europe. That day the canopy provided welcome shade, the silence broken only by my stumbling feet. Ahead the path snaked down between the trunks, quietly disappearing in the peaceful air.

Peaceful, apart from the pilgrims. My self-esteem took a further knock as I was overtaken by a cheerful young couple, chattering away, the man carrying their two-year-old on his back while the woman toted the family's belongings. I perched on a boulder to let them bounce by, but generally there was nowhere to stop: on and on I zigzagged, my knees clicking and complaining, my poles scrabbling for purchase on the interminable shale. It would be days before I developed the technique of using the poles as extra limbs, much of my weight on my arms, stalking swiftly down rough tracks like some hunchback mantis.

Hours later I scrambled down to level ground and found myself facing a daunting stone wall. Despite its forbidding appearance I had reached shelter. At the vast *albergue* in

Roncesvalles, developed from a twelfth-century monastery, chilled out, fitter pilgrims chatted in the afternoon sun. I stood rooted in the entrance hall, swaying and footsore, my head swimming with fatigue and achievement.

"Yes, we have a bed for you," confirmed my Dutch host (many hostels are manned by volunteers, often former pilgrims, returned to minister to those who follow). "But your pack needs adjusting. There is too much weight on the shoulders. You should be able to pass the hand under the straps." Good advice, but surprisingly tricky: I tugged and slackened for the next month.

The complex in Roncesvalles features a wonderfully modern dormitory, laundry, and bathrooms − I did not at that point appreciate just how valuable this was − next to a swish hotel for better-heeled, if not better-shod, travellers. Feeling righteous, I glanced dismissively at the hotel's elegant furnishings and returned to my spartan (but entirely adequate) pale pine bunk.

History seeps into every pore on the Camino. The twisting paths and ancient stones of St Jean had warned me, but in Roncesvalles the past tapped me on the shoulder.

For a start, the chapel of the Holy Spirit adjoining the hostel is constructed on an ancient pilgrim graveyard. According to legend, it also marks the burial ground of part of Charlemagne's army. Charlemagne and his men had been given free passage south by the people of neighbouring Pamplona, in exchange for assurances that the city would be left in peace. On their return northwards, however, the marauding Franks badly damaged the city walls, and in response the disgruntled Basques massacred their rearguard. It was during this skirmish that Roland blew his horn, too late, and the *Chanson de Roland* was born.[18]

Legend may have its facts wrong, since Charlemagne's incursion into Muslim Spain happened over 300 years before the chapel was constructed, but clearly memories ran deep in these mountains. I resolved not to break any promises to Basques.

---

18 A long and bloody epic poem based on the Battle of Roncevaux (Spanish: Roncesvalles) in 778. It is the oldest surviving major work of French literature, composed before 1115. In the poem the ambush and massacre are blamed, quite inaccurately, on the Muslims whom Charlemagne had gone to fight. Roland, covering the rearguard, refuses from pride to blow his horn to summon help; too late, he blows with all his might, whereupon his temples burst and he dies a martyr's death.

Why?

You cannot walk the Camino without tripping over history. But why? Why did the impulse towards pilgrimage flower so strongly after the turn of the first millennium?

Shortly after AD 1000 there was, particularly in France and Italy, a sudden rush to rebuild churches. It was part of a period of spiritual intensity, which also gave rise to a rapid increase in monasteries and would eventually lead to the Crusades.

At that point there was undoubtedly in Europe an onset of some form of millennium fever. This was not necessarily a matter of fear: to oppressed, poor, disease-ridden men and women the possibility of Christ's imminent return was to be welcomed.

However, the critical date was not the turn of the century so much as the period covering the next thirty-three years, running up to the thousandth year since the passion, death, and resurrection of Christ. The true millennium, therefore, was not the year 1000, but rather the anniversary of Christ's departure.[19]

The expectant atmosphere in monasteries, courts, and at the tables of the reflective seeped out into the wider

---

19 Tom Holland, *Millennium*, London: Abacus, 2008, p. xxv.

population, engendering a culture of mingled hope and desperation. There were visions, and much preaching. It was a febrile period, in which tenuous faith grew firmer.

At the same time a more peaceful political climate rendered travel a little easier. In the ninth and tenth centuries raiding parties of Vikings, Arabs, and Magyars had pillaged the gold- and silver-encrusted shrines of Western Europe (one consequence of which was that the fleeing monks of Lindisfarne exhumed the famously intact body of St Cuthbert and wandered with it across Northumbria for over a century before settling permanently in Durham). But at the end of the tenth century a series of separate military victories across Europe gave Christian rulers control of land routes to the Holy Land, and once-impossible journeys became merely extremely difficult.

These two factors – a rising spiritual hunger across Europe, and the opening up of key routes – ushered in the Age of Pilgrimage.

In the eleventh century there were several mass pilgrimages, from Normandy, Aquitaine, and Burgundy in particular. The fate of the Holy Places aroused a good deal of enthusiasm in these provinces, and in 1024–25 an "immense leaderless mob" of pilgrims left for the Holy Land.[20] Such unpredictable, spontaneous revivals dot Christian history, and can leave a considerable legacy – for instance, many of today's vast and teeming congregations in Latin America, and elsewhere, are Pentecostal in origin, a movement that began in Los Angeles and takes its point of departure from

20 Jonathan Sumption, *Pilgrimage*, London: Faber and Faber, 1975, p. 119. I am indebted to Messrs Sumption and Holland for many of the facts in this chapter.

the Azuza Street Revival of 1908. It is possible to make the case that the widespread impulse to pilgrimage was at root a true movement of the people, an awakening prompted by the Spirit.

Yes, *but*. Years of labouring in the vineyard of Christian books have confirmed that motives are rarely unmixed. At one Christian trade fair in Denver, I overheard a snatch of conversation in a queue for lunch:

"This is a great deal."

"Yes. Let me pray about it."

You sort of knew the outcome.

Anyone who makes their living from their faith is inherently compromised. For no one is this more true than for vicars, ministers, pastors, priests. Their house, their income, their sense of self, their family's security, their pension plan, their social position – all derive from their calling. This is not to imply that the majority of ministers of religion are charlatans, but under the circumstances it requires an extra degree of integrity to pay Richard Dawkins, for example, the attention he deserves, and to chase down the hares of doubt he sets running.

I am one of the compromised, of course.

In ferreting out motivations from a thousand years ago it is incumbent to bear this caution in mind. Whatever the presenting reason for undertaking a pilgrimage, a host of subsidiary motives come along for the ride.

The worldview of the medieval pilgrim was one in which the daily intervention of God was the standard explanation. A fine harvest? The Lord was smiling. A wife infertile, or a child stillborn? You had failed to do penance.

A red sky at night might speak of war. A partial eclipse of the sun foretold disaster. A flash of lightning became the punishment of God. From the most trivial to the most vital events of human life, God was in charge and the material world was the arena of spiritual conflict. Excessive importance attached to specific events. Fear was your daily companion: fear of malign spirits; fear of displeasing the Almighty; fear of overlooking an obeisance to a saint.

With such a charged view of action and consequence, you tiptoed through the world. Dreams were the open doors of the mind. Evil sprites thronged the dark air, seeking possession of the sinful. Death surrounded you, your own death the stuff of sermons. Damnation lay across your path – and scoffers beware: the pains of hell are all too vivid. The damned, according to Richard Alkerton of London in 1406, will be "boiled in fire and brimstone without end. Venomous worms… shall gnaw all their members unceasingly, and the worm of conscience shall gnaw the soul."[21]

It is hard to see things in the same way as our forebears. Today we readily believe in progress, the possibility that tomorrow will be better than today. Our entire economic system is based on credit, which is a glib way of saying that we are borrowing from the future, which is OK because the future can afford it: who knows what new technologies may arise? A thousand years ago there was no such conviction: the future was neither bright nor orange; the past was better than the present; whatever happened was out of your control; your overlord did not invest to secure future production, but

---

21 Sumption, *op. cit.*, p. 20.

spent his wealth to demonstrate his magnificence and ensure fealty.[22] This side of the grave there was little prospect of improvement or advancement. Your father died in poverty; so would your son.

In this profoundly pessimistic, fearful, and fatalistic culture, pilgrimage offered a valuable safety valve.

For a start, there was the possibility of miracles.

Miracles were the surest validation of a shrine. Medieval men and women considered miracles to be part of the texture of life, the natural operation of things. Pilgrims offered prayers at their chosen shrine above all for healing, their own or that of a cherished spouse or offspring, leaving a token of appreciation – or supplication – in the form of a leaden arm, or head, or foot. The practice continues today: in Greece I once found a small boutique in the lee of a church with bowls of body parts for purchase by the faithful.

Many shrines were careful to verify the accounts of miracles. Despite this, Thomas More, councillor and chancellor to Henry VIII, held that most such stories of miracles were fraudulent. The reformer John Hus claimed that clergy paid beggars handsome sums to wander from town to town announcing they had been cured at the shrine of Wilsnack, where three communion wafers survived a fire that consumed the church and village in 1383.

The age of pilgrimage certainly had its share of pretenders. But every major shrine had amongst its staff those whose job it was to record the most spectacular miracles in collections of stories called *libelli miraculorum*. This is a practice dating

---

22   For a crisp analysis of the rise of capitalism, and the mindset that preceded it, see Yuval Noah Harari, *Sapiens: A Brief History of Humankind*, London: Penguin Random House, 2014, pp. 341 ff.

back at least to the time of St Augustine (AD 354–430), who collected depositions from the pilgrims healed by St Stephen at Hippo. These accounts were then included in Augustine's sermons and circulated in neighbouring dioceses. The classic collection, widely esteemed in the early Middle Ages, was made by Sulpicius Severus in the fifth century and concerned the miracles of St Martin. This set the dreary pattern for many later records, which then as now seem to have been notable for their repetitiveness.[23] There are few new books under the sun.

Let me not sniff too loudly. The man who regained his sight, or the barren woman who conceived, the sick child who against all odds recovered: these were potent evidence of the efficacy of your selected saint. The rationalist in me wants to dismiss these many, many stories as simple fabrications of a credulous age; but – quite apart from the danger of patronizing intelligent men and women worthy of respect – I still today find a ready appetite for tales of healing. And I have wandered the beaches of the sea of faith for far too long to be easy with automatic scepticism. Faith is not just for the pointy-headed. The existence of an organization such as Christians in Science (or its US equivalent, the American Scientific Affiliation), which includes many of our most brilliant scientific minds, should give the lie to comfortable doubt.

It is one thing to read stories of miracles, which can quickly pall. You tend to be able to guess the punchline.

It is another to watch them yourself. Many of the students at All Nations prayed in their money (the fees

---

23 Sumption, op. cit., p. 151.

were modest, but most were poor, and overseas students struggled with the exchange rate). It was a daily thrill to stand near the pigeon holes as my friends opened unanticipated envelopes with whoops of joy. In this respect at least the worldview at All Nations would have been quite familiar to a medieval pilgrim.[24]

So would another practice current across the UK today: that of street prayer. In one Kentish town some friends of mine set up a screen and chairs in the High Street (having scrupulously obtained permission from local officialdom) and offered to pray for passers-by. Some crossed the street, others scoffed, but still others accepted, and were duly followed up by the church in question. "We've seen some fantastic stuff," said my friend Sheila. "Not just physical healings, but reconciliations, marriages saved, lives turned around."

The local agnostics set up a table nearby to distribute dissenting leaflets, but this wonderfully British response petered out.

To the medieval mind, hunger for the miraculous was not a means to a quick spiritual thrill. In an age of frequently ineffectual medicine, the aggravations provided by worms, parasites, toothache and gout, diseases and epidemics and famines – the ordinary agonies of life – led to a fatalism where only the spiritual offered relief. A bad harvest meant starvation. War meant starvation. In a world of tight margins, taxes might mean starvation. Shockingly bad roads might mean starvation, too, while neighbouring provinces struggled

---

24   I decided at one point to compile a volume of stories of "All Nations miracles", but lost heart for the project after the distressing news about my daughter.

to store surplus crops. Even when none of the above applied, the deficiencies of much of the medieval diet, often short in vitamins and highly seasonal,[25] meant that to feel completely well may have been quite rare. And since physical ailments were believed to have spiritual causes, a pilgrimage might reasonably be offered as a pledge in exchange for future wellness or the recovery of a beloved child.

One common ailment was ergot poisoning, sometimes called "St Anthony's Fire" (named after monks of the Order of St Anthony who were particularly successful at treating the condition) and caused by eating bread made from rye infected with a mould, *claviceps purpurea*. Outbreaks were common after a wet summer, leading to considerable numbers suffering from severe burning, gangrene, convulsions, fever, mania, and psychosis. The condition sparked some notable mass pilgrimages, and certain shrines on the Santiago route gained a reputation for healing the afflicted, possibly because well-run monastic economies ensured clean grain, and sufferers in monastery hospitals enjoyed a more wholesome diet – or, equally possibly, because the drier southern climate inhibited the mould.

---

25 It would remain so for centuries to come. Medieval farming practices involved a two-year rotation, with land being left fallow or turned into pasture, a practice which allowed the earth to recover some fertility, but which meant a low output and many lean months.

[Just for interest: The introduction of the four-year crop rotation method, notably including clover and turnips, was pioneered in Britain by the agriculturist Charles Townshend in the eighteenth century. The system (wheat, turnips, barley, and clover) generated a fodder crop and grazing crop, allowing livestock to be bred year-round. The four-field crop rotation was a key development in the British agricultural revolution, and substantially increased output. The addition of clover and turnips allowed more animals to be kept through the winter, which in turn produced more milk, cheese, meat, and manure, which maintained soil fertility.]

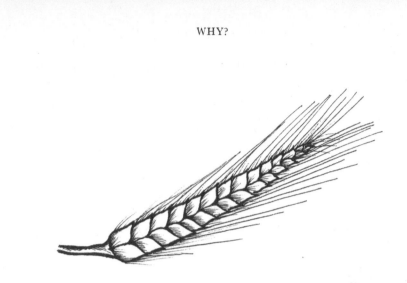

In a world of medical insurance, to so confidently link spiritual and physical seems wacky. Less alien in some contemporary circles, however, is another expression of the same conviction, that sickness can be caused by sin. The fall of man, it was widely held, had given Satan authority over the bodies of men as well as their souls. Only by remaining in a state of grace, therefore, could a man preserve his health. John Chrysostom, Archbishop of Constantinople (AD 347 −407) held that "sin is the first cause of bodily disease". Accordingly, it was thought possible to vomit up the devil, and infection could be explained as the physical transfer of a demon from one body to another − a belief with a parallel in the story of the Gadarene swine (Mark 5).

In such a world there was considerable tension between the church and medical profession, which offered to heal without reference to the spiritual. A synod meeting in Paris in 1429 actually forbade physicians to treat any patient in a state of mortal sin. Jewish doctors, as heathens, were particularly shunned: if the sickness lay in the soul, how could a Jew be of service?

While shrines were praised for their efficacy in healing, they were scarcely transportable. This snag gave rise to the practice of collecting dust from particular shrines, which was then applied to the afflicted area. More highly prized still was water from the Jordan. As then, so now: in Jerusalem I have watched fervent ladies pouring water onto marble tombs, then mopping the slab with handkerchiefs and squeezing the liquid carefully into plastic bottles.

There are two altogether more prosaic attractions to the idea of pilgrimage.

The first is simple: the pull of the open road. Like Everest, you climb it because it is there. To be a pilgrim is a simple thing, but huge. It dominates the landscape. It defines you. On the road, you walk. Your destination is not in question.

This makes everything easier. Your choices are minuscule but immediate – where to eat, where to sleep. Your pack may weigh you down and your feet may hurt, but the road grants freedom.

The second attraction is separate, but related. By setting foot on the pilgrim trail you are released from the web of status and commitments that dominates everyday life. Ambitions and fears can be safely set aside. The towns through which you pass may salute you, and sell you a meal or a bed, but you and the townspeople both know you will be gone in the morning. There is no obligation to pursue any relationship or to continue any conversation. Your acquaintanceships may last an hour, or a day. You may walk with others for a month, or six, but you are not their neighbours for life. Even if you (like many of my companions) opt to plug your iPad Mini into the Web at every passing bar, you are still removed from your natural habitat.

I quickly dropped into the daily habit of texting my wife with an update, and treasured the contact.[26] But that was all. She and my daughters alone knew how to reach me. Despite the shared facilities of morning and night, you are a solitary individual in a world where solitude is rare. I loved it.

---

26 She kept an eye on the map of Spain, and with Google Earth could sometimes see the same sights.

Burguete — Larrasoaña
Day 3

That night in Roncesvalles I ate the first of many pilgrim meals.

Every restaurant on the Camino seems to offer a menu *peregrino*, featuring pasta. The refectory that served both hostel and hotel was not an inspiring introduction. The rough red wine was frankly horrible, but improved when poured into the insipid *potage de légumes* (a trick learned in youth, when I had spent a year teaching at a French school).

In the dinner queue I fell into conversation with Nicole and Paul, French pilgrims. Nicole was a slim, vivacious woman in her early fifties, short-haired, short-skirted, and buoyant. Paul was a tall, skinny guy in his late forties. In constant pain from a wrecked back, he carried his enormous pack strapped to his chest, peering over the top like a crab. Intensely devout, he was completing a few days on the Camino as his job allowed, stopping frequently to pray at wayside chapels. He would keep us company for a couple of days before his inner turbine compelled him to surge ahead, and we saw him no more.

Paul's strong regional accent and voluble speech, punctuated by incomprehensible witticisms, proved a challenge to my rusty language skills. Nicole, calmer and clearer, was far easier to follow, and over the next few days we spent hours in conversation. She had already walked over 1,000 kilometres, setting out from Le Puy in central France. Her husband, a baker, had died a year or so previously of a heart attack, and she was undertaking the Camino at least in part to prove to herself that she was back on her feet. She was indeed, and a swift lady too: ruefully I had to accept that this Frenchwoman – not so much younger – was a good deal fleeter than me.

A pilgrimage is not a race. Really. It doesn't matter who comes before or behind, how far you have walked that day, how many days you take overall. The journey is the destination.

I repeated these observations as a mantra, right across Spain. The seed fell on stony ground.

I am inherently competitive, obsessed by numbers, a scrutinizer of league tables and bestseller lists. I cannot follow sport: I care too much. When driving I hate being overtaken, and the red mist lurks at my shoulder. In traffic jams I have to hold myself back from switching lanes obsessively. On the Camino you carry your quirks with you, and time after time I caught myself lengthening my stride – I can take that guy in the next mile – or casting anxious glances backwards.

How utterly absurd. It's *not* a race, I told myself severely, as I demonstrated yet again all the self-mastery of a puppy chasing a car. I repeated to myself the wise lines from Max Ehrmann's *Desiderata*:

> If you compare yourself with others, you may become
>   vain and bitter,
> for always there will be greater and lesser persons than
>   yourself.

It didn't work. It would be weeks before I could convince myself not to reach for a higher gear.

Anyone with the first smattering of Christian understanding will be chuckling in pity by this point. What happened to the first shall be last, and the last first? To the doctrine of grace freely given? You cannot earn your place in heaven; you cannot win a pilgrimage.

The following morning Paul, Nicole, and I were on the road right early. It was still pitch black, cold, with a heavy mist. The café where we had intended to breakfast was shuttered and dark. The way wound between large trees, the path full of roots to trip the unwary.

I had a torch, but searching for the vital yellow arrows that mark the route is a challenge in the dark, so it was with a sense of relief that we found a café on the outskirts of Burguete willing to feed us coffee and *tostada*. Other pilgrims trooped in after us, and when we stood to leave we had to extricate our possessions from a pile of packs. I soon learned to keep an eye out for a scattering of rucksacks betokening a functioning watering hole.

Give thanks for Don Elías Valiña Sampedro. Don Elías (1929–89) was the parish priest in O Cebreiro (O-Thay-Bray-Aero) in Galicia, and a student of the Way of St James. He set himself the challenge of reviving the route and in 1984 put in motion his mission to rescue, clean, and mark the trails along the Camino, starting in Roncesvalles. He it was who initiated the practice of painting the iconic yellow arrows to indicate the right choice at the various crossroads along the trail. Legend has it that Don Elías drove across the whole north of Spain, his Citroën GS packed with yellow paint. It is entirely possible that without him the Camino would today be little more than a memory.

Today yellow arrows pepper the route, offering a comforting nudge to the errant traveller. Sometimes the arrows are augmented by representations in stone or bronze of the *coquille St Jacques*, the scallop of St James. At every juncture where an inattentive pilgrim might stray, yellow streaks daubed on tree, rock, kerbstone or wall set you straight. If the arrows disappear, retrace your steps. I found myself giving thanks day after day for our unnamed guides and their pots of paint.

In the modest, tightly packed town of Burguete, as the light strengthened around us, we fell into company with Alain, a tall, bluff Frenchman. Alain was full of the experience of the previous night, when he had stayed in the Hotel Burguete, a hostelry formerly patronized by Ernest Hemingway, who not only visited regularly but had been persuaded to sign the piano in the bar. Hemingway, an aficionado of bull fighting, particularly relished the annual running of the bulls through the streets of nearby Pamplona, at the Festival of San Fermin (he actually fought a bull himself at the amateur *corrida* in 1925). His novel *The Sun Also Rises* celebrates the bull running, and so provided a considerable boost to the local economy – a favour returned when Pamplona's leading hotel opened in 2009 under the name *Hostel Hemingway*.

As we left the outskirts we passed a notice about the witches of the area, and I shivered. In the sixteenth century a number of wise women were classified as witches, and burned in the town square. Despite Alain's cheery anecdotes, I found myself imagining those very dark days and regarding the inoffensive burghers of Burguete with unease. I found it hard to shake off the sense that there was a stain on the town.

During the years at All Nations I started to take the spiritual world a good deal more seriously. For many, spirituality is a closed book, best classified in your internal Dewey system under Piffle, between Pan, Peter, and Potter, Harry. My own scepticism is deep and automatic. Yet – how can I put this? – when I pray I have a suspicion that Someone is listening.

If there is Light, must there also be Dark? By temperament and conviction I give little credence and less time to the agents of his Infernal Majesty. I am no fan of horror movies, and séances spooked me badly on the few occasions of undergraduate experimentation.

Nevertheless I have had the odd brush with the dark side. All Nations students were divided into teams and allocated to work with churches in the locality. This was excellent on-the-job training. One team, however, found they could make no headway at the village church to which they had been assigned. Relationships went sour. Books vanished. The minister suffered from debilitating depression. On hearing this, my Scottish surgeon friend nodded grimly. "There are two covens in that village," he informed us. After that revelation we prayed, extra hard, whenever our friends headed off for the village in question, and gradually things improved.

Most mainstream churches take the issue seriously. In the Church of England the House of Bishops issued a set of guidelines for deliverance ministry in 1975, which was reviewed and reissued in 2012. There is a priest in each diocese with particular responsibility for exorcism. Catholic churches in Italy and Spain are training more priests in the work of exorcism,[27] in response to a rise in occult activity.

Nevertheless, looking back on that episode I feel queasy. My early confidence that witches are self-evidently bad has been replaced, partly by greater understanding of what is involved in serious paganism (in which there is much to respect) and partly by a far sharper awareness of the countless crimes that have been perpetrated by the ignorant against the enquiring.

In my imagination smoke still swirled around the eaves. I was pleased to leave Burguete behind.

---

27 Reported in *The Independent,* 8 January 2014.

We padded quietly through the drowsing town and at the Banco Santander veered sharply right, over the cheerful Rio Urrobi and onto a wide farm track. And, with the daylight now bright upon us, we were walking through a pleasingly green arable farmscape: we could have been in Surrey. Within minutes the town and its grim history were invisible behind us, and we started to develop a steady pilgrim stride. Paul and Nicole kept up a cheerful banter for a while, then fell silent. Alain, our Hemingway enthusiast, set a rollicking pace, and was soon out of sight.

As the previous day, the path wound through woodland: to a high point, the Alto Mezquiriz, then precipitously down to the Rio Erro, briefly up then down and down again, a steeply gravelled descent to the Rio Arga and the small town of Zubiri. At the medieval bridge into the town, wherein lay several hostels, Nicole and I paused briefly, but it was barely 2.00 and, feeling bullish, I resolved to press on to Larrasoaña. The bridge, the Puente de la Rabia, deserved more attention than we gave it. It is averred that any animal led three times around its central column will be cured of rabies. Evidently it was a place of healing: Zubiri itself is the site of a former leprosarium.

Zubiri would probably have been semi-deserted, like most of the other villages we would pass through in the days ahead, if it were not for the vast, angular, extraordinarily ugly and dust-shrouded Magnesitas plant that straddles the valley ahead. As we walked over the brow of the hill, with Zubiri at our backs, colour drained from the landscape: within a few paces the roadside brambles, the spiders' webs, the rocks, the trees, the path ahead, all seemed to have been thickly dusted with flour.

Magnesite, magnesium carbonate, is used *inter alia* to line blast furnaces and in the manufacture of synthetic rubber. It is sometimes used in the treatment of cardiac patients, and in caring for those with a low magnesium level. It's very useful.

I have the skimpiest awareness of the industrial processes that sustain me, and the grim factory I passed that day discouraged closer acquaintance. A licensed tree hugger, I am acutely embarrassed that my profession requires wood pulp, and every garden I have owned has featured more trees when I left than when I arrived. I love the earth, viscerally and profoundly. It would not greatly upset my equilibrium if I never visited another church, never sang another hymn. But to fell a tree foolishly, and more acutely to kill a beast unnecessarily, fills me with grief and fury. An elephant is a walking hymn of praise: how can anyone shoot it for its tusks, to make trinkets for tourists? To buy extra beer, to strut your stuff – or any more affluent equivalent – at the expense of a devastated land, such as the Alaskan tar sands, is crass beyond words. Progress can be very ugly.

To compensate for my part in our profligate society I try, quite hard, to live lightly upon the earth. I am part of a household of five adults, and living together cuts costs and minimizes our joint footprint. Pen and I eat little meat, usually organic. We heat our house in part from a vastly efficient wood stove. Our roof sports solar panels and solar thermal tubes. We feed, daily, the local foxes and badgers, crows and herring gulls (who are not above tapping on our windows when their servants are tardy with the scraps). We keep our possessions pruned.

Yet the industrial world is my daily bread: I drive a desk; I publish books printed on reconstituted trees; I cover 25,000 miles a year in my frugal hybrid. So you may call me a hypocrite, hopelessly compromised, and I will bow my head. Shame is part of my being.

It may have been a necessary part of the world economy, but that Magnesitas plant was a terrible scar on a beautiful landscape. As fast as my pack, my increasingly painful feet, and my internal conflicts would allow me, I strode on by.

And came at length to the medieval settlement of Larrasoaña and its Albergue Municipal. Again I stood swaying in the doorway, and gave my details to the smiling lady custodian (one of the consistent pleasures of the Camino is the unfussy but kindly welcome from those who manage the *albergues*). I bagged a bottom bunk – such meanness of spirit – parked my walking poles, and profited from the cold water sinks in the courtyard to do some laundry. It had been a long, hot day, and my uncomplaining canvas bush hat, purchased years before in the Rockies, was drenched in sweat. As I luxuriated in a shower (individual cubicles, but like many bathrooms and most dormitories on the Camino, the facilities made no concessions to gender), I started to get a grip on the realities of pilgrim life.

The pilgrim has no privacy at night, though the road offers solitude. You take turns at the loo, the showers, the cold water taps where you wash your clothes. You sleep in dormitories, usually in bunks, sometimes a hundred to a room. You retire early, because you are knackered. You rise early, because some idiot is peering under their bed with a flashlight in search of socks.

During supper – at a table in the town's main bar, crammed shoulder to shoulder with loud and cheerful pilgrims – I sat next to one of the very few Englishmen I would meet on my journey. A prosperous young banker, he was briefly between jobs and had reserved a bare four weeks to accomplish the entire route to Santiago. In order to undertake the pilgrimage, he told me, he had left his wife and children behind, and I raised an eyebrow in his direction. Could he not do it in stages, and take his time, as so many do, and perhaps enjoy the company of his family? No, he responded categorically: he had a timetable.

I gave him credit for the courage and vision to snatch even this brief respite. But I felt sad for the driven executive, and sad too for my own high-pressure choices. So much effort. So many distractions. It had taken me far too long to discover the flavour of silence. I greatly wish I had undertaken my first pilgrimage in my twenties, rather than my sixties. I have come late to the joy of the road, but *tant pis*: under the Mercy I intend to return.

That night I collapsed into my bunk well before lights out and – according to Nicole – snored like an ungreased mill wheel right through the night. Nine hours, poof.

Pamplona – Cizur Menor – Puente la Reina

Days 4 and 5

The following morning I trudged off alone, while nimble Nicole and turbo-charged Paul forged ahead. Instead I enjoyed the tranquil forested path along the Rio Arga, relishing the stillness and pausing to admire a little scurrying lizard. At the top of a hill a kindly Korean girl offered me blackberries. In the next village I rested my pack on a low stone wall. An Israeli stopped to chat, and shared chocolate. The day had started well.

In my path lay Pamplona, of running bulls and Hemingway fame. Even in non-fiesta mode it is a bustling place, a university city with strong ties to the Camino. Hemingway memorabilia include a statue outside the bullring. There are endless shops selling trinkets, and a very bull-oriented culture. You can buy your eager nephew or niece a pair of mock horns mounted as handlebars on a single bicycle wheel, a purchase for which every parent will thank you.

"Be prepared for the noise and bustle of city life after the relative calm of the Camino," cautions Brierley. "City folk are forever in a rush, so tread warily amongst the traffic and watch your wallet."

My cards and cash were secure, my moneybelt well concealed, but I found the abrupt plunge into urban Spain disorienting. I was still painfully unfit, and that day's 13-mile stretch drained my resources. The Camino runs right through the centre of the city, and I paced with aching bones past bus stops and municipal buildings and the imposing Universidad de Navarra, feeling utterly out of place, a figure from history, despite the frequent "*Buen Camino!*" from the hospitable Pamplonans. I had been walking surrounded by space, a traveller in another realm, and to be thrust back into a busy European city was an assault. I trod doggedly on, following the bronze *coquilles St Jacques* let into the pavement – no gaudy yellow arrows in this sophisticated spot.

I negotiated the gleaming centre and the shabby suburbs. There were *albergues* to be found in the city, but I wanted something quieter. I dragged my pack and weary limbs over the bridge above the Rio Sadar, climbed the valley out of Pamplona, and by 3.00 p.m. had arrived in the hamlet of Cizur Menor, where I found a berth at the Albergue Roncal, a private hostel with a garden and very welcome bar. We had not prearranged it, but on the sunny terrace I found Nicole and Paul. Such serendipitous encounters are a joy of life on the Camino. Lazily chatting, and intermittently translating for an Irish couple (Bernadette and Mike, whose daughter worked in Bexhill, 5 miles from my home), I sat and sank several beers and watched pilgrims trickling in, sweating and weary, demi-humans seeking showers.

The days were starting to fall into a routine: arrive, register, get *credencial* stamped, shower, wash clothes, recuperate, dine, sleep. In the early morning you gather your possessions, checking under your bunk with a torch for errant socks, apologize to your sleepy neighbours, and as surreptitiously as possible roll your sleeping bag and stuff it into its pocket. Rub Vaseline into your feet, retrieve the T-shirt you have left drying on the end of your bed, frantically search for and with relief locate your boots, disentangle your walking poles, shoulder your pack, and set off into the dark dawn to find a café catering to the pilgrim trade.

By the second week, as the season advanced, I would begin each day torch in hand, searching anxiously for yellow arrows.

The next big test was the formidable Alto del Perdon, the Hill of Forgiveness, which Nicole and I tackled the following day. Abrupt and rocky, it looked insurmountable, but in fact was barely half the height of the summit of the Route Napoléon. Before we started to climb, however, we crossed the innocuous and peaceful expanse over which Charlemagne's army defeated Aigolando's Muslims in the eighth century. Northern Spain is a land of blood.

From the hostel at Cizur Menor I had spied the wind turbines that lined the high ridge to the southwest of Pamplona, and over breakfast Paul gave me the French term: *éolienne*, after Aeolus, Greek god of winds. The back of my notebook was rapidly filling with recondite French vocabulary.

They looked close, but the distances were hard to gauge, and conversation ceased as we struggled upwards through the scrubby woodland along the wide rocky route.

We had been warned to look out for the dry well where, according to legend, a medieval pilgrim had collapsed, dying of thirst. The devil, disguised as another pilgrim, offered to show him where to find water on condition that he renounced his faith. The devout man refused, and St James himself most wondrously appeared, giving him to drink from a scallop shell. "Today the well is dry," comments Brierley portentously, "a sign perhaps of the spiritual aridity of our times."

I record this comment because it annoyed me. By any standards it is simply untrue. Professor Richard Dawkins may have gleefully proclaimed the vanishing of his cardboard deity (I must not be unfair: his work has given a tremendous boost to the sale of Christian books, and Christians everywhere owe him thanks for generating so much interest in the interface of science and faith), but the idea that spirituality is dead is simply preposterous.

Churches in South America, sub-Saharan Africa, and Asia are growing rapidly: in England the cathedrals are seeing significant growth in attendance,[28] and the Fresh Expressions movement has generated the equivalent of no fewer than four additional dioceses in the Church of England alone.[29] Over 20 million people have attended Alpha courses around the world, of which 2.5 million in the UK. British Roman Catholicism is seeing a strong boost, in part thanks to inward migration from Eastern Europe. Spanish-language churches in the States are growing at a startling rate. And that is just a glimpse of the Christian world.

---

28 According to one report, a quarter of the UK's population visits a cathedral every year.

29 This is a fast-moving situation. Check out www.freshexpressions.org.uk.

There are some interesting quirks as spirituality makes a comeback: Jews for Jesus, an evangelistic group, reports that as much as two-thirds of its growing congregations are from Gentile backgrounds.

The cheerful assumption of the "new establishment", as Sean Oliver-Dee[30] has termed them – the usually London-based journalists, politicians, and sociologists who dominate the public's media diet – is that religion, and particularly Christianity, is little more than a phase in the rise of the secular state. But this is a serious error, not least because it blinds policy makers to the obvious: the fact, for example, that you cannot engage with the interplay of forces in the Middle East without regard to religious patterns of thought. Canon Andrew White, often tagged the "Vicar of Baghdad", has warned time and again of this profound error, a trap into which many a military leader and diplomat has fallen. Andrew, who is trusted by rabbis, imams, and bishops alike, exemplifies how to do business in this perilous environment.[31]

For a fuller exploration of the whole issue, see the excellent and entertaining *God is Back* by Micklethwaite and Wooldridge, two journalists from *The Economist* magazine.[32] For up-to-date information on important religious stories, see the excellent Lapidomedia site.[33]

---

30 Dr Sean Oliver-Dee, Fellow of the Royal Historical Society, is Research Fellow at the Centre for the Study of Religion in Public Life at the University of Oxford, and author of *God's Unwelcome Recovery* (Oxford: Monarch Books, 2015).

31 See *The Vicar of Baghdad* by Andrew White, Oxford: Monarch Books, 2009.

32 John Micklethwaite and Adrian Wooldridge, *God is Back*, London: Penguin Books, 2010.

33 www.lapidomedia.com.

Leaving the world picture aside, the enormous renaissance of the Camino itself must suggest that something is happening. Much of the widespread spiritual activity is unfocused, oblique, unrelated to any formal credal system. But it is certainly not arid.

We didn't find the well. But there was no avoiding the *éoliennes*. The enormous structures filled the clean air with their beating as we laboured towards the summit, stepping round gasping cyclists and their panniered machines. As we crested the ridge the harsh October wind suddenly hit us, and we stumbled into a crowd of pilgrims congratulating themselves and photographing one another.

Along the north side of the ridge stand tall wrought-iron silhouettes of pilgrims and their horses – a dramatic sight, but a sad temptation for passing graffiti artists.

As we started down the steep and crevassed opposite slope I switched my poles experimentally to a pencil grip, supported by the wrist bands, and immediately found that this answered better. Transferring much of my weight to my arms I was suddenly striding, leaping swiftly downhill from boulder to boulder, a rush of exhilaration after the days of trudge. For once Nicole was left far behind, stepping cautiously. Hah.

My joy continued, but my incipient self-satisfaction was abruptly punctured as a tall guy with a shock of long curly grey hair came *running* past me down the neck-breaking slope. I had noticed him two nights before in our dormitory, a wiry gent in sleeveless T-shirt and cut-off jeans, fit and muscular. As I stared in astonishment after him, watching as his pack bounced with every stride, he turned a kink in the track and in moments was out of sight.

That was my first encounter with Mack, the Marine no longer on active duty. He ran 37 kilometres that day.

We came across a café in the village of Uterga and stopped for a drink. The Camino is dotted right along its length with free fountains, and pilgrims are warned frequently to top off their camelbacks. But, for sheer thirst-quenching delight, I have to confess that on the Way I became a Coke addict. The sudden burst of sugar and caffeine was just what my body needed. Normally, in dear old Blighty, I cannot stand the stuff (my father once trenchantly referred to it as liquid toothpaste, and I concur). But to a weary pilgrim it was nectar and ambrosia in a handy can.

My dietary requirements and tastes were changing. Normally, as my cholesterol levels remind me whenever I fall off the health wagon, I am given to applying butter with a trowel; cheese and pâté, the more odiferous the better, speak to me in seductive tones, and I am a sucker (or would be, if a bout of heart disease had not issued me with a lifetime ban) for any generous combination of salt and fat. What I don't greatly relish is sugar. Cakes do not induce drool, biscuits are a fleeting temptation at most, and open boxes of chocolate are reasonably safe in my custody. I drink my coffee black.

Now everything changed. In addition to regular Coke stops, I found myself starting every morning with a strong milky coffee thick with sugar, chasing down the dawn Ibuprofen to dull the pain in my cranky limbs before the steady rhythm of the day took control.

Meanwhile my fat intake was falling away. A pizza with extra cheese left me queasy; the salad option looked tempting. The morning *tostados*, served with a meagre pat of butter that would once have set me calling for the waiter, now tasted great with jam. I was learning to listen to my body – which, to my quiet satisfaction, was starting to get a little, the merest smidgeon, thinner. He is a happy man whose trousers seem loose.

I was starting to adapt to the daily demands, growing slightly less soft. So when Brierley's guide recommended a detour to the curious church at Eunate, I accepted the challenge.

Churches, as buildings, do not really appeal. I am not blind to sublimity, but drab years of being dragged churchwards by parents indifferent to a child's Sunday morning bilious attacks have left their scar on the soul.

However, the twelfth-century Church of Santa Maria de Eunate merited the side trip. Its octagonal form closely resembles the Holy Sepulchre in Jerusalem, and speculation links it with the Knights Templar. A delicate golden brown, it stands alone, apart from a little nearby hostel, surrounded by open fields and low grey hills. It serves no community, hosts no regular worship, has no obvious reason to be. Yet for centuries it has been a place for pilgrims to halt and pray, and sometimes die: archaeological excavations have found many burials, and the tell-tale *coquilles St Jacques*.

What appealed to me was its austere beauty, the complex form completely unadorned. When Nicole and I pushed open the heavy weathered door and entered, it took a moment for our eyes to adjust to the near-darkness within. A man and two girls sat on the bench that circled the little church, their packs leaning beside them, listening intently to a quietly playing CD of Gregorian chant. Abruptly hushed, we found our own seats, grateful for the cool and sombre stone that surrounded us, and gave ourselves over to silence, underlined by music.

In my experience God doesn't say much. But sometimes it is possible to listen. It is one of the gifts that churches offer. As you settle and breathe, amid distant voices, half-sensed cars, the wind outside, you may find a space of your own. Your heart slows and your mind roams. You have a tiny part to play in the dance of the atoms, the great slow wheel of the galaxies, the gentle tick of the future becoming past.

I had hoped that God might have something to say to me on my journey. In this enigmatic place, a tonic to the spirit, He simply said: *stop*.

Much refreshed, we walked on, browsing as we went – walnuts, almonds, blackberries, apples, grapes, plums, all overhung or lined the route and rendered the placid countryside an open larder. More than once, spotting a grim-faced farmer in the distance, I had to encourage Nicole to move along. But in truth much was going to waste, vineyards abandoned, apples unplucked.

Later that day we made it to Puente la Reina and the Albergue Jakue, a pilgrim hostel occupying the basement of a tolerably lavish hotel. The brisk young woman seated at the welcome desk under a leafy arbour sold me a beer in an ice-crusted glass, straight from the freezer, and told me where we could wash our clothes.

Her English was fluent, so I asked if she spoke Basque. The language had sparked my curiosity: every sign appeared in both Spanish and Basque, and I had passed a bookshop in Pamplona full of books in Basque. Yes, she said: she and her school friends had learned it in class, and spoke it with their grandparents. Her parents, like so many, had turned away from their ancestral tongue, or had been forced to do so by Franco's nationalistic policies, or simply by the need to find work. Yet now a combination of schooling and adult education is gradually re-establishing Basque as a living language – like Welsh, a language of choice: there are practically no monolingual Basques.

I asked our young host what she spoke with her friends. Spanish.

After supper that night we wandered down the racketing N-111 and into the centre of Puente la Reina. The outskirts were drab and semi-derelict, but then Nicole laughed and pointed upwards. On the summit of an old freestanding wall, mere yards from the furious main road, clustered an immense bundle of twigs. That late in the year the storks were long gone, at least from that corner of Spain, but they had left their homes plain to see. We spotted more nests that evening on a church bell tower, and in the weeks ahead they would become a common sight, even lodged precariously on cranes and bits of farm machinery.

Storks are known for migrating south from Europe to North Africa to overwinter, but these days many thousands are staying in Spain, and particularly Portugal, all the year round. Powerful opportunistic birds, they congregate on rubbish dumps much like seagulls in Britain.

The astonishing bridge over the powerful Rio Arga is at least part of the reason for the town of Puente la Reina.[34] The *Reina* in question, Doña Mayor, the wife of King Sancho III of Navarre, commanded that it be built, and financed its construction. Six elegant arches wide, it was completed a decade or so after the turn of the first millennium to provide a crossing point for the many pilgrims who converged on the site, for Puente la Reina is where two *caminos* meet: the Camino Frances, originating in Paris, and the Camino Aragones, which starts in Toulouse and crosses the Pyrenees further to the east.

A keen supporter of the Benedictine abbey at Cluny, King Sancho III (c. 992–1035) was a busy and practical monarch. His primary contribution to the burgeoning world of pilgrimage was to improve the road from Gascony to León. Sanctity and commercial nous in one crowned head:

---

34 "Bridge of the Queen"

this road would bring increased traffic down to Iberia as pilgrims flocked to Santiago. Because of this, Sancho ranks as one of the first great patrons of the Way of St James.

There is a *correos*, a post office, in the centre of Puente la Reina, and pilgrims I met that night were sorting and selecting items to mail home. I conducted a mental inventory, but apart from an overly pessimistic medical bag there was nothing superfluous in my pack. Pity.

That night in Puente la Reina brought a flood. The hostel occupied the basement of the hotel, and a bath above had overflowed, or a sink had blocked. The entire dormitory was woken at 3.00 a.m. by the sound of rushing waters and sleepy staff in pyjamas clanking around with mops and buckets. Several beds were drenched, and those who had stuffed their packs beneath their bunks found a nasty surprise the following morning. The mess was eventually cleared and exhausted pilgrims collapsed back into slumber, but it was a very unwelcome two hours. My only damage was a wet hat, so I had little to complain about.

However, it was also a night for dreams. The first few days of the Camino had ended in spectacular nightmares, the kind from which you wake screaming, and this night was little better: an episode so grim (it unfairly involved my first wife, a friend from Sevenoaks days, and a house fire) that I recorded it in my journal, along with a much happier dream involving an insolent chattering carful of *Today* programme presenters.

I was bemused by these dreams. Normally such visions of the night pass harmlessly through my brain, after the manner of the Augean Stables, leaving calm and order in their wake. But this was different, and the chimeras had set their claws in me night after night. It was as if a violent spiritual enema were being administered. The common quality of these recurring nightmares was that I had failed, thoroughly, unforgivably, in the most obnoxious way, endangering my daughters and letting down my friends. The life of a pariah was too good for me: turn your face aside, lest you be infected.

In fact Puente la Reina would prove a turning point: there would follow several nights filled with dreams of unusual buoyancy and cheerfulness.

Puente la Reina – Estella
Day 6

The next day's walk, a relatively level and benign affair, took us through gentle hills and farmland, only notable for the medieval bridge crossing the Rio Salado, the Salt River. This stream features in an account compiled by the rather splendidly named Aymeric Picaud, a twelfth-century French monk and scholar, who assembled what is now called the *Codex Calixtinus*,[35] an illustrated manuscript offering advice to travellers – in essence, the earliest known guidebook about the Way. This provides far more than tourist information, and includes sermons, accounts of miracles, liturgical texts, and early polyphonic musical pieces along with lists of useful vocabulary, descriptions of the area, works of art to be seen en route, and notes on local customs. The original is now housed in Santiago Cathedral.

The *Codex* runs to five volumes, and in the Age of Pilgrimage it proved a popular read, playing its part in the rising reputation of St James and the establishment of his

---

35 It was formerly attributed to Pope Callixtus II.

shrine as a focus for pilgrimage. Almost half the material is given over to liturgies and homilies relating to the saint, with two accounts of his martyrdom. The last volume contains practical advice for pilgrims, informing them where they should stop, relics to venerate, sanctuaries to visit, bad food to avoid, and commercial scams of which to be aware, including other churches that claimed to hold relics of St James.

Aymeric Picaud was not impressed by the locals he met, and records the following incident:

> At a place called Lorca, to the east, flows the river known as the Salt Stream.
> Be careful not to drink it or water your horse there, because the river is lethal. On its banks, as we were going to Santiago, we found two Navarrese sitting there, sharpening their knives, waiting to skin the horses of pilgrims which die after drinking the water.
> When we asked, they lied and said the water was safe to drink. So we watered our horses, and two died at once, which the men then skinned.[36]

He did not have an easy time of it, poor man: a later note in the *Codex* dourly records, "All fish, beef and pork in Spain and Galicia make foreigners ill."[37]

---

36 https://sites.google.com/site/caminodesantiagoproject

37 With reason. At one point I was conducting a week's seminar, on aspects of marketing, in Brazzaville in the Democratic Republic of Congo, and by the second day my intestines were fighting back against the indigestible local diet. Since I was the principal speaker this was not a matter my hosts could ignore, and at my urgent request they instructed the kitchen staff to prepare for me nothing but vegetables: a swift and effective remedy – with biblical warrant in the story of Daniel, moreover.

That day the Rio Salado was a modest trickle. We crossed safely, free of equine concerns, and set our faces to the west. We stopped for a snack in the little village of Lorca, then as we ambled on through the dusty autumn countryside, we heard the sound of singing.

Round the corner towards us strode a cheerful – actually, ecstatic – French lady of middle years, her voice raised in a hymn of praise. We stopped to chat and learned that she, like Nicole, had started her pilgrimage in Le Puy, in central France. She had made it to Santiago, and was now on her way back, this time heading for Lourdes. I looked at her in fascination: I had rarely seen anyone so totally, completely happy. She waved goodbye, and as she disappeared over the ridge behind us we heard her voice lift again.

She was virtually the only black person I would meet on the Way.

Ahead lay Estella, founded in 1090 by Sancho V, King of Navarre, who saw the commercial (and, lest we impose an inappropriate cultural template, the spiritual) potential in the rising stream of pilgrims. Stonemasons and artists were invited to take up residence, and the result is a borough still notable for its fine buildings and bridges. However, its history is marred by local rivalries, and by the oppression of its Jewish minority – a vigorous Jewish colony was rooted out cruelly and entirely in the fourteenth century. Unlike Burguete, however, I could sense no overhanging miasma.

On that occasion Estella was notable for its weather. As we approached the outskirts rain started falling for the first time since I had landed at Biarritz. Within minutes it was hosing down, and we scampered across the dark stone of the glistening bridge and up through the narrow streets in search of the nearest hostel.

When we signed in, I noticed that our host was a dwarf, and we quickly realized something slightly wonderful: the hostel we had chosen so arbitrarily (the Albergue Anfas) was run for and by people with disabilities. A sweet but silent young woman with Down's Syndrome showed us to our bunks and explained in gestures how to find the washrooms and operate the laundry. Since the few minutes of heavy rain had left us drenched, we set to work washing, wringing, and spreading to dry every garment we had been wearing.

It was Saturday night, and Nicole wanted to attend mass. The downpour had eased to a drizzle, and as we emerged into the stone-scented, dripping dusk we discovered Estella in fiesta mode. At the bottom of the high street stood a little stage, where a vigorous mariachi band, strident in red, was doing its very best to lift local spirits, the amplified voice of the singer booming through the damp air. A modest crowd sheltered under the shop awnings opposite. We edged on by after a few minutes, and in the centre of the town Nicole pointed to an imposing sweep of steps. She was absolutely right; at the top we turned into the Iglesia San Pedro, a twelfth-century church where the kings of Navarre once took their vows.

The nave was dimly lit, encrusted with gold-leafed statues and redolent with wood polish and incense. Despite my utter ignorance of Spanish I could follow much of the service, as it closely paralleled the Anglican communion. At the conclusion Father Jean Michel pronounced a special blessing on the twenty or so pilgrims who had attended the service, offering greetings in English, French, Portuguese, and

Japanese and quizzing us all on our backgrounds and hopes. I shook hands with two lads from Brisbane. "When you stand before the cathedral of St James," said Father Jean, "please say a prayer for Jean Michel, parish priest of Estella."[38] He handed out copies of the Prayer of the Pilgrims, which can be found at the end of this book.

Feeling frazzled after the long day and the lengthy mass, we found our way to a crowded nearby soccer bar, where a cheerful waitress served us utterly delicious stuffed peppers, a local speciality. Peppers – pimientos – are widely grown, and are usually dried, or charred and preserved; a day or so later I found one jolly couple roasting a mountain of red bell peppers on a large barbeque beside the road, and handing out plums to passing pilgrims. Strings of peppers hung drying in every town we passed through.

On the way back up the hill we noticed a number of solid-looking barricades being set in place along the edges of the street. A bartender confirmed something I had not previously appreciated: the running bulls of Pamplona are just one manifestation of a much wider regional custom. The bulls themselves were scheduled to put in an appearance the following day, and I was tempted to stay and watch, but neither of us relished being stuck in the town for the length of a Sunday ("Everything shuts," explained our friendly barkeep).

A few minutes later we came across something I would rather not have seen: a crowd of young men and boys tormenting a bull calf on a long rope, leaping to one side as the poor creature lunged. Spain suddenly reminded us

---

38 I did.

we were strangers: in Britain such cruel entertainment, and worse, occurs of course, but not in the middle of a street party.

Shortly after that we found ourselves back in front of the mariachi stage, where the band was still operating at joyous full volume. The crowd had now greatly increased, milling around, waving bottles and calling to one another. We were enchanted by a couple of tiny girls with their parents, both exquisitely dressed in local costume. Nearby stood a large model bull on wheels, garlanded with firecrackers and Catherine wheels, clearly intended as the culmination of a forthcoming display.

A few moments after we had returned to the hostel and settled down for the night, the most almighty bang shook the air, rattling the windows. The bull had been wired, I suspect erroneously, to explode all at once.

It ain't easy, being a bull in Spain.

Estella – Los Arcos
Day 7

The following morning the track out of Estella was damp, but as the day lightened the walking grew easier. I was eager to sample the free wine fountain outside the town, provided since 1991 by the Bodegas Irache, the Irache Wine Cellar.

There seems something utterly wonderful about a wine fountain, a sheer liberal-handed open-hearted joy. A hedonist to my very core, an oenophile of little sophistication but great enthusiasm, this completely floated my boat. Who cared that this was shrewd business, and that every passing pilgrim now knew the brand? Here were free samples on a grand scale.

I love the generosity of God. It is one of the reasons I have remained a believer, and a servant of Christ, for so many years. One of my favourite passages of the New Testament comes from Luke 6:37–38 (NIV):

> Do not judge, and you will not be judged. Do not condemn, and you will not be condemned. Forgive, and you will be forgiven. Give, and it will be given

to you. A good measure, pressed down, shaken
together and running over, will be poured into
your lap.[39] For with the measure you use, it will be
measured to you.

This chimes perfectly with the doctrine of grace: of divine
favour freely given; of the loving Father who attends to the
flight of the sparrow. Our God is an exuberant God, who
made the earth and saw that it was good:

Come, all you who are thirsty,
come to the waters;
and you who have no money,
come, buy and eat!
Come, buy wine and milk
without money and without cost.
Why spend money on what is not bread,
and your labour on what does not satisfy?
Listen, listen to me, and eat what is good,
and you will delight in the richest of fare.
Give ear and come to me;
listen, that you may live.[40]

This accords easily with Jesus' injunction to recalibrate our
values:

So why do you worry about clothing? Consider the
lilies of the field, how they grow: they neither toil
nor spin; and yet I say to you that even Solomon in
all his glory was not arrayed like one of these.[41]

---

39 Christ was probably referring to the way the outer garment was worn,
leaving a fold over the belt that could be used as a large pocket.

40 Isaiah 55:1–3, NIV

41 Matthew 6:28–29, NKJV

It is not always easy to perceive the good. A part of my work as a publisher is to discern what is of the Spirit. Every day new proposals arrive, new ideas emerge. Which ones merit the felling of a tree? A tree is itself a fine upstanding psalm of joy: will God be more pleased if I turn it into a book? And so, every day, I pray for guidance and wisdom as I open the morning's crop of emails.

It is, sometimes, a little easier to discern what is not so good. Every so often I come across a book – sometimes a well-argued book with real commercial potential – that I try to walk away from. Perhaps it will be an exposé of the errors of the Jehovah's Witnesses, or of the New Age. Perhaps it will be an attempt to codify the laws of Christ, or to explain why men should have headship over all women, or why the environmental movement (or the World Council of Churches, or homosexuality, or the Conservative Party, or tarot cards, or astrology, or liberal theology *passim*) is of the Evil One.

Such books have their place – I believe very deeply in freedom of speech – but I want nothing to do with them. Christians should denounce hypocrisy (starting with themselves) and fight hard against injustice, but the Servant King did not spend His time rooting out heresy and neither will I. It is simply far more important to affirm what is wholesome, and true: to promote what is good, rather than to expose error. Error will die away; good will remain.[42]

This also applies in the area of fiction. I rejoice in the redemptive potential of story, and enjoy publishing novels that serve the truth. Such books not only uplift the reader; they teach him or her to discern what is worthy of praise.

---

42 This is not to imply that the World Council of Churches, etc. are of the Evil One. Really.

It is a task incumbent upon Christian teachers, pastors, preachers, to assist their listeners to be more discriminating in their consumption of our culture. If this TV drama, that film, that book makes you feel better, more sober, clearer in your mind, more sure-footed in your capacity to be a better friend, parent, lover, colleague, then that drama or film or book has done a job worth doing. If the drama promotes envy, or fosters hatred, or teaches a superior attitude, or sows cynicism, or inflames lust, then who is blessed? Discover those works of art that help you walk the road of blessing.

And, in my universe, a judicious sampling of a fine vintage helps to gladden the heart. When I first learned of the wine fountain at the Bodegas Irache, my spirit leapt, just a little. OK, so it was barely nine in the morning: red wine was on offer.

The reality slightly disappointed. The wine *tap* ("fountain" is stretching it) is set into a wall behind the winery, and it offers the patient pilgrim the chance to fill a hastily emptied bottle with an entirely drinkable fluid. The tap emits a steady, constrained trickle, and after waiting my turn I half-filled my enamel mug. Standing at the edge of the eager crowd, I took a couple of mouthfuls.

It was agreeable enough, and at the end of a long day, seated in some old stone refectory, accompanied by fresh French bread, unsalted butter, and a well-matured brie, it would have been perfectly palatable. As I perched at the edge of the path, the temperature rising and my sullen rucksack gnawing at my shoulder blade, it was not the greatest drink to foster the pilgrim soul. So others found too: in the next hamlet stood a pair of Coke bottles under a plane tree, half full of wine, abandoned at the side of the road.

Stepping carefully round a sextet of inebriated ageing Spanish day-pilgrims who were dancing a joyful rumba up the path, Nicole and I adjusted our packs and set a steady pace up and out of the valley.

Shortly after the wine fountain the route branched, offering pilgrims a more moderate route flanking the N-111, or the tougher and far steeper "natural" road. Choosing the scenic route, however, involved a long, unpopulated, unwatered stretch of track, and once we emerged from the extensive forests of oak and pine which flank the town of Estella, the day burned bright and hot. I stopped to dig the sunscreen from my pack, but my southern neck, arm, and leg were already red. Over the ensuing days I would acquire a wonderfully partial and lop-sided tan, a true case of lorry driver's elbow.

The road was starting to grow, frankly, boring. Scrub, or fields of sunflower stalks. Almost no one around, except other pilgrims; nothing to watch, except other pilgrims. Thoughts turned inwards.

I had developed the practice of commissioning a *bocadillo*, a sandwich of tomato and chorizo, often liberally sprinkled with oil, from whichever café served me breakfast. Some time around elevenses we sat on the parapet of a small (and probably medieval) bridge, and with our mouths full gestured a cheerful greeting with our snacks at those who passed us.

By early afternoon we had reached Los Arcos, a small crossroads town, and the small and delightful Casa de la Abuela, a private hostel run by a young family. Washed and refreshed, we made our way into the central square and there espied a familiar group.

As the days rolled by a steady cohort of pilgrims, perhaps a couple of hundred, were becoming our daily companions on the road. The same faces would recur: sometimes a spurt of energy, or an injured foot, would affect the mix, but again and again we recognized our fellow travellers.

So it proved now. From an outdoor table we were hailed in an unmistakeable brogue, and a few minutes later, beers in hand, we joined a turbulent Irishman called Brian, whom we had first met in Roncesvalles. A lecturer in psychiatric nursing, Brian epitomized the "crack", and had an inexhaustible fund of stories about the music world in Liverpool and Dublin. With him sat a grim and formidable Finn, whose name I failed to discover, who had been a UN soldier and who regaled us with alarming tales from the

Golan Heights. Yarning is currency on the Camino, and while we sat and swapped tall tales, several Americans were attracted to the shouts of laughter. Some of the new arrivals were limping from quite horrible injuries – mainly neglected blisters – which they resolutely ignored. In the following days my half-remembered St John's training and my overstuffed medical pack would be pressed into service.

As the evening drew in we started looking for a suitable restaurant. One of the regular frustrations of the Camino is that you follow a different time frame from that of the local population: at siesta time you are still miles from your billet, striding away; by six o'clock you want to eat and sleep, while restaurants are barely unbolting their doors. With a little persistence we found a table; by the time we were finished, the café we had chosen was alive with bustle and noise.

That evening a particular tension came to a head. Nicole had crashed out ahead of me, and as I stood in the communal bathroom cleaning my teeth, a tall American lady turned with a raised eyebrow and observed, "I see your little girlfriend has already gone to sleep."

Ouch.

Nicole had been excellent company, and we had found much to talk about. But I had already become aware that I did not want to walk right across Spain in the company of a lady other than my wife. There was no misunderstanding between us: Nicole had a boyfriend waiting for her back in Le Puy. Nevertheless, I had allowed a friendship to develop that was giving the wrong signals to our companions. The Camino can accelerate friendships, and our fellow travellers had leapt nimbly to the wrong conclusion.

I am a friendly cove, mostly, and enjoy conversation. I can be ebullient, and like a laugh. As a bumbling idiot of some standing I have managed to upset, annoy, and mislead too many women by misplaced friendliness. Discretion and reticence: I can spell them, but they are not always in my repertoire. Spaniel, wagging tail.

Now I flushed hot with embarrassment. Long after lights out I turned the matter over in my mind, and realized there was no way round it: we would have to stop walking together. I felt like a heel, unkind, clumsy, and oversensitive.

The following morning Nicole, mature and sensible, instantly grasped my stumbling concern and volunteered to set off ahead of me. With relief I watched her leave – she would easily outpace me – and with a feeling of a crisis survived set about buckling my pack and finding my boots. We would encounter one another occasionally, but she would reach Santiago a day ahead of me, and go on to Finisterre.

This is such a minefield. I try, really hard, to behave with propriety in all contexts, to be friendly and open, but not to intrude. Again and again I get it wrong. I suspect, from the occasional candid conversation with male friends, that I am not alone. The world is full of plonkers.

Despite a strong sense that I had behaved badly I was relieved. I could hardly have managed the matter less elegantly, but I did want to be alone, to be silent, to give myself time to think and pray.

It was not until much later – after my return – that Pen pointed out that "girlfriend" has a less loaded meaning in the States.

Torres del Río – Viana – Logroño
Day 8

That morning I faced – alone – a formidable segment of the route, with a sharp hill and a much longer stage. Brierley suggests that you take it over two days, to allow time to explore Logroño, over the horizon, and because the road is demanding: "Shade is limited to a few isolated pockets of pine and drinking fonts are few."

Quite apart from the tough day's walking ahead, something else was becoming apparent: my large but inexpensive pack was starting to generate real grief. Two metal rods formed the core structure, and one of them had poked through its little pocket, rendering the whole thing unstable. Once I discovered this I freed its companion, which meant that the pack simply sagged, rather than lurching wantonly. Furthermore the buckle on the critically important waist strap (which allows you to carry the weight on your hips, not your shoulders) was starting to give way, popping out if I moved incautiously – springing lithely over a puddle, for instance. This, I told myself ruefully, was why wise folk spent serious money on a good backpack. Saggy, smugly awkward, unbalanced, and not even waterproof despite its bright orange rain cover: useless. I had no one but my cheapskate self to blame.

On my return home I Freecycled the lumpy thing, and bade it farewell without affection.

In Torres del Rio, the first of the day's settlements, I stopped for a coffee in a bustling café, busy with pilgrims, and spotted Alain, my Hemingway enthusiast. He was seated at a little table beside the window, by himself, wolfing down a vast platter of fried sprats. Nicole had told me a little of his history: not only had he survived colonic cancer, he had undergone a double heart bypass the previous year, and – feeling that his card was marked – was now gathering every rosebud. A knowledgeable gastronome, he was full of details about the local dishes, and intent upon tasting all. Now he cheerfully waved a fish at me in response to my shouted greeting. Shortly afterwards he passed me as we climbed the steep hill outside the village, waved again, and disappeared ahead.

At the top of the hill I came across a slender iron cross, its base festooned with donations from those who had preceded me – photos, messages, plastic knick-knacks, scarves, a rusty watch. As I stood for a moment to pray, I was disconcerted to find tears brimming in my eyes. Wayside shrines on the Camino are often decorated like this, and my snotty younger self would have regarded such folk religion with condescension: blind men seeking they knew not what. Now I realized that I, the pilgrim, was the one who had not seen: this was not ignorant superstition, but a natural and unforced reverence. I could no longer stand apart from the people, commenting and commissioning comment. I was a pilgrim too.

Brierley's guide is effusive about the historical and cultural wonders to be relished along the Way, and each night I would read up on what to spot the following day. So when I reached Viana, a fine golden medieval town of arches and deserted courtyards, I stopped to view the tomb of Cesare Borgia, who had been killed nearby.

Young Cesare, born in 1475, was the son of Pope Alexander VI, and brother of Lucrezia Borgia.[43] Bishop of Pamplona at age fifteen, he was made Cardinal at eighteen when his father ascended to the throne of Peter. Shortly thereafter he created ecclesiastical history by being the first to resign the cardinalate, when on the death of his elder brother (Captain General of the papacy's military wing, who was assassinated in the traditional mysterious circumstances) he took up arms and was granted in turn the command of the papal armies – Italian mercenaries supported by French troops. After two notable military successes against Italian towns, he was accorded extra funds – made available when his father created twelve new cardinals – enabling him to acquire the services of several *condottieri*, professional warlords. With these forces he imposed his authority on the Papal States of Romagna and Marche, and, given the venality of the rulers he ousted, he was welcomed by the harshly oppressed locals.

An immensely capable general and statesman, adroit and – when necessary – ruthless, he was nevertheless dependent on his father's powers of patronage. After the latter's death Cesare was chosen by the historian and politician Niccolò Machiavelli as an illustration of how a ruler can suffer if acquiring a principality through the power of another – though the author of *The Prince* praises some of Cesare's more treacherous acts. His father's death spelled the end of Cesare's rule of the Papal States.

A skilled war leader, he spent much of his brief adult life

---

43 The indefatigable Pope Alexander had six offspring, and was the first pontiff to openly recognize his children born out of wedlock.

in military excursions. He met his end in 1507 when laying siege to the castle of Viana, having captured the town. Some knights had escaped from the siege, and Cesare furiously gave chase, distancing himself from his troops and dying when his intended victims turned on him.

I read the history and inspected the tomb.[44] Cesare was a man of anger and blood, an enthusiastic adulterer (he fathered at least eleven illegitimate children), and not above using treason as a weapon of statecraft. Yet the inscription on his original tomb read, in translation: "Here lies in a little earth he whom everyone feared, he who held peace and war in his hand. Oh, you who go in search of worthy things to praise, if you would praise the worthiest then your path stops here: you need go no further."

Most of us appreciate a good scoundrel. It is no different in the world of Christian books, though the added narrative of redemption is *de rigueur*. An early example in my experience was Charles Colson, US President Richard Nixon's special counsel in the years leading up to the Watergate scandal, and widely regarded as Tricky Dicky's hatchet man. He was once quoted (inaccurately, but it was readily believed) as saying he would drive over his grandmother to get Nixon re-elected. A former captain in the US Marines, Colson was a tough, intelligent lawyer, ruthless and decisive, described by David Plotz in *Slate* magazine as "the evil genius of an evil administration".

---

44 Originally erected within the Church of Santa Maria in Viana, the tomb was thrown out later in the century by an indignant bishop, and Cesare's bones were reburied in the main street, where all might tread upon them. In the twentieth century the bones were exhumed, identified and, years later, finally rehoused in the entrance to the church.

In the months surrounding Watergate, with criminal charges levied against him, Colson made a brave and astonishingly ill-timed decision: he became a Christian,[45] pleaded guilty to a relatively minor charge, and was promptly jailed by a judge conscious of the world's sceptical gaze. His conversion was ridiculed, of course, but Colson's time in prison proved a turning point for the now-disbarred lawyer: he became personally, vividly aware of the many injustices perpetrated by his country's justice system, and on his release founded Prison Fellowship, a group dedicated to the care and rehabilitation of offenders. He bent his great abilities to the new cause, and in 1993 would be awarded the million-dollar Templeton Prize for progress in religion (he gave the money to Prison Fellowship). He was also awarded fifteen doctorates. The world that had execrated him gradually took him to their hearts.

On his release he wrote a bestselling and surprisingly entertaining book, *Born Again*, with the assistance of co-authors John and Elizabeth Sherrill.[46] Hodder & Stoughton published the UK edition, and as junior editor and gofer I carried Colson's bag from one launch event to another. One morning Hodder's managing director Eric Major described with relish how he and Colson had been plotting strategy in the back of a cab the previous night. "He hasn't changed that much," said Major, grinning. "We agreed what had to be done, and then Colson turned and looked at me. 'We have a saying in the Marines,' he said. 'Get them by the b****, and their hearts and minds will follow.'"

---

45 After reading *Mere Christianity* by C. S. Lewis.

46 Authors of *The Hiding Place, The Cross and the Switchblade*, and many more. Their books, mostly written on behalf of others, have sold millions.

Standing at Cesare Borgia's tomb, I thought they would have found something to talk about.

As the stony pilgrim track approached the city of Logroño the surface changed to drab-coloured asphalt – easier on the ankles but painful to the soles. The local government had done this thing, and I mourned the improvement, which drained that stretch of road of its meagre charm. All along the Way I would come across many such investments, some sensible, others looking suspiciously like a resourceful appropriation of EU funds – the Way is a European heritage route. Stands of inexpertly planted, resolutely neglected, and peacefully dying trees are a common sight.

Despite these depredations, nothing could disguise the significance of the conceptual border I now traversed: I was entering the autonomous region of La Rioja – that magnificent fount of some of the richest reds in Europe – and raised a mental glass to my absent colleagues. I crossed the powerful Rio Ebro on the wide stone bridge, constructed in 1880, which replaced the original instigated by San Juan de Ortega (St John of the Nettles, presumably in reference to his rural background) in the twelfth century. San Juan was an early civil engineer, a great friend to the Camino, and a tireless and inspiring builder of roads and bridges. Yet again the pilgrim tribe was creating its own durable infrastructure.

I leaned for a moment over the parapet, hoping to see a fisherman, but no joy. Although the world, books, family, and church have too often edged this passion off my timetable, I am at heart an angler. Nothing terribly highfalutin; I am a simple fisher of coarse fish, and most of my childhood was spent on some river bank.

In every tackle shop I have ever visited, the proprietor or a fortunate patron will have proudly pinned up a photo of himself hugging to his bosom one of the Ebro's utterly enormous catfish.

Erase from your mind the delicate bewhiskered chappies you may find in tropical aquaria. The Wels catfish of the Ebro are monstrous brutes, top predators, up to 6 feet in length, cunning, voracious, and immensely powerful. Ugly wide-mouthed grey creatures, they draw specimen hunters from all over the world. Fishy stories are common wherever anglers congregate, but have you heard about the catfish that caught a pigeon? Not a duck – that would be fair enough – but a *pigeon*? Check it out on YouTube.

Across the bridge I found myself abruptly in the narrow labyrinthine streets of the medieval quarter and, offered a bewildering array of possible hostels, chose the generically named Albergue de Peregrinos, which turned out to be clean, welcoming, and possessed of abundant hot water. I washed myself and my clothes, sat on my bunk, and wrote up the day's experiences, ending with the following hostage to fortune: "My appetite is surprisingly slight. One evening meal and a snack for breakfast and lunch seem sufficient."

How holy. So very pilgrim, my dear. Perhaps I was becoming spiritual after all.

With a frisson of pleasure I donned the lightweight shoes I had purchased in Hastings; weighing just a few grams, but with thick protective soles, they were ideal for a night on the cobbles. They verily caressed the feet. Thus shod, and with my pack stowed beneath my bunk, I could have danced across the city.

Pilgrims become very swiftly obsessed with feet. Your choice of boot, shoe or sandal is critically important, and every guide and website I broached in preparation had sternly warned of the importance of breaking in your footwear. Soon after my pivotal conversation with Douglas, the cleric who had turned my face towards the Camino, I had invested some serious money (far more than I spent on my benighted rucksack) in a pair of top-of-the-range boots, and a valuable investment they proved.

Feet are a topic of conversation at any hostel. People you have met minutes previously are all too willing to bare their soles. There are many pharmacies along the Way, and without exception they carry generous displays of Compeed plasters, ointment, and needles. The poor assistants in these shops are called upon with disagreeable regularity to prescribe medicaments and pronounce upon some ghastly injury, the offending limb hauled into view and propped on their clean counter.

I had another reason to focus on feet. Occasionally, over the last couple of decades, I have fallen prey to a bout of gout. Uric crystals, with their affinity for the ball of the foot, can create an agony whose particular acuteness is unlike any other pain I have so far encountered. An attack can come on quite swiftly, even mid-motorway, and on occasion I have driven home screaming. My colleagues have grown used to my turning up from time to time nattily attired in carpet slippers. An attack while on the Camino would have rendered the whole enterprise void.

Occasionally a lady will fall subject to gout, but at least 95 per cent of the world's complainants are male. It is supposed to be brought about by over-indulgence in women and fine wine, but my example refutes this.

So, on the Way, I took my allopurinol tablets with strict regularity.

Then there was the question of socks. After some experimentation and investment I had struck a good balance: polyester inner socks, which do not retain moisture, beneath proper hiking outer socks composed of wool, nylon, and Lycra.

This combination served well enough on the hills of Sussex, and worked tolerably on the Way, where I was walking on harder surfaces and over much greater distances. But the best solution of all I would never have expected.

The afternoon before I left for Biarritz, Pen and I drove across to visit her mother, who had grown up on a farm, and still has family in Yorkshire. With some ceremony she presented me with three pairs of alpaca socks, provided by a niece with a flock of the beasts, which she had commissioned specially. I accepted them, I hope with grace, but slightly reluctantly, having weighed every item to the gram.

Yet these were to prove the best of all: comfortable, soft, durable, and, unlike the hi-tech hiking specials, they didn't draw the feet. Two weeks into the Way I texted Pen: "Tell Grandmary alpaca socks rock!"

Now I washed my friendly footwear and hung them up to dry, glad they had found a place in my pack.

In fact my frenetic weight-saving had gone too far. I could not let the days pass without a photographic record, especially now Nicole and her camera were no longer on call. The girl at the hostel desk gave me directions to the appropriate store, where I was able to purchase a compact affair in lurid purple, and scanned the instructions in Spanish and Urdu.

Taking pity at my gormless expression, the salesman deftly set it going. Thereafter it was rarely out of my hands.

As I emerged from the camera shop I realized I had skipped lunch. My earlier burst of energy suddenly gone, I wandered wearily back through the dusk, negotiating the prosperous teeming streets, staring sidelong at the tapas bars,[47] and finally settling for a steak sandwich. Abruptly ravenous, I attacked it with a will.

Emerging somewhat refreshed, I took my new toy for a stroll and ran into the Irish contingent I had met in Roncesvalles and again in Los Arcos – Brian, Pat, Bríd, plus a cheerful Australian woman who turned out to be a TV chef Down Under. They made me welcome, and we settled down to some emerald banter. I am one-eighth Irish,[48] from my mother. A clout with the Blarney stone is no bad thing for an editor.

A beer or so later, as the darkness descended, I joined them at a street restaurant for a further full meal. So much for asceticism. Hold the admiration.

I believe I mentioned that the Way had entered La Rioja? At the end of September, right when I and my fellow Irish were broaching a third bottle of the good stuff, the festival of San Mateo kicks off in Logroño, which explained the crowds. This festival celebrates the grape harvest in a weeklong cheerful frenzy. If we had been tourists we would have stayed and lent our support to this quaint local custom. But we were pilgrims, and, eyes set upon the hills whence cometh, we bid the revellers farewell and wandered bedwards.

---

47 Over fifty in the city centre, each specializing in one or two dishes. Logroño is something of a culinary capital.

48 Seven-eighths mongrel.

Logroño – Nájera
Day 9

amera in hand, and once again alone, I set off into the dawn. Today's was another long stage, but I was in good spirits. The first few photos show lumpy objects shrouded in mist and glistening bronze and gold in the streetlights. I snapped an unsuspecting street cleaner, braced against his water cannon, directing the jet into every cranny, sluicing detritus down the sloping alleys, carrying away the cigarette butts, lager cans, fish heads, broken glass, newspapers, and syringes of the night. Logroño rises each day to a dawn of sparkling cleanliness.

La Rioja is known for its rich red soil, which in the autumn sunshine warms the landscape and gladdens the pilgrim heart. That day it rained solidly, all day, and by ten in the morning the track was glutinous red mud, embracing my boots with enduring affection.

That lay ahead. I paused at a café in the suburbs for a *tostada* and strong white coffee, staring blankly at the pretty TV presenter above the counter and gathering my forces. Fumbling a painkiller from my pouch – paracetamol had become part of my morning routine, allowing me to stare down the aches and twinges of the day – I downed it with a gulp, paid, nodded to the proprietor, and turned to go.

The Spanish, basically, do not do breakfast. Every morning, blearily stumbling to life, I would seek out a bar and order whatever unappealing offering was available: a dry croissant, a plain cake, a chocolate doughnut, washed down with white coffee heavy with sugar.

Few things separate the nations as much as their breakfast habits. As a language assistant at a school in France I had rejoiced in the early morning crusty bread, accompanied by strong coffee. Americans seem to blend health and heart disease effortlessly in a single plate, strawberries and melon slices sitting primly alongside waffles drenched in syrup and sweet whipped butter. German hotels – though this may be Teutonic humour at the expense of English guests – seem to top their breakfast *würst* with rollmop herring: after eating a German breakfast you know you are awake, with that particular clarity engendered by too much pickled fish. For Spaniards the matter is simple: breakfast, in my tiny experience, was a foreign contrivance, to be regarded with as much suspicion as, for example, sticking to the speed limit.[49] Once, in the course of the Camino, I discovered a shop selling muesli, in very small packets, at very high prices.

The drab suburbs behind me, the clouds lifted, and I padded for a while alongside a wonderfully clean and elegant lake, the Pantano del Grajera, which serves as reservoir for the city. I have the same affinity for lakes as I do for rivers: they make the soul sing. Beyond it the track follows the rising

---

49 To be fair, this is something of a challenge: Spain has a speed code of impressive complexity.

hillside, up to the high point of Alto de la Grajera; looking back you gaze over the lake with the city at its back.

Or would do, should the weather permit. As I reached the summit the sheets of rain closed in again. Before I left Britain I had purchased a poncho widely reviewed as the best available, a thin but voluminous garment roughly the size of the O_2 Arena that envelops you and your pack and can be secured between the legs in the event of a modesty-challenging tempest. It folds to a tight wad and weighs less than a kilo. A stick and a few pegs will transform it into a bell tent; with a satisfactory heat source it could double as a balloon.

It also served as an ambulant sauna, and could be donned only with the aid of an assistant. Now I enlisted the services of an amused Italian girl, clapped my dripping bush hat back on my dripping scalp, scrambled up through a grove of pine trees, and set my face towards Nájera.

At the peak of the Alto de la Grajera the track runs between two stretches of motorway, and is bounded by chain-link fence. It's an unlovely spot, but right along the path pilgrims have set up crosses, dozens of them, woven into the fence, comprised of bark, branches, and scraps of cloth. The crosses run for several hundred yards.

Before setting out someone had asked me why I was undertaking the Camino, a question with many possible answers. Taken off guard, and trying to be both brief and candid, I replied, "To look for sources of reverence."

Now, like a military cemetery, the crosses ranged before me, stretching out ahead as far as the curve in the track. I ambled past them lost in wonder, stopping occasionally to admire some particularly elegant or unusual creation. This was the work of many seasons, the devotion of many hands. I would encounter the phenomenon again and again as I walked through Spain: a piece of utilitarian fencing transformed into art, and an act of worship.

As the track moved out into open country I paced between neatly cultivated vineyards still heavy with fruit. Yielding to temptation I filled my mouth with the sweet grapes, hoping the farmer would not miss his fraction of a litre.

A few kilometres before Nájera the path passes through the outskirts of Ventosa, a small village chiefly remarkable for its history: it is situated close to the Poyo de Roldán, Roldan's Hill (a variant of Roland), where our hero slew the Muslim giant Ferragut with a deftly thrown rock and liberated the Christian knights of Charlemagne's army. One feels that the chronicler might have had David and Goliath in mind. Ventosa was yet another symbol of the deep historical enmity between Christian and Muslim in this land: a theme that would recur. Coming from multi-cultural Britain, where every town has its mosque, and Muslims play a valuable role in government, this constant dripfeed of buried hatred upset and offended me. Call me gullible and naïve, but surely it is time to move on.

After all, the Normans invaded England a thousand years ago, and who remembers the Battle of Hastings?[50]

By the time I arrived in Nájera it was late; I was damp, and weary. The poncho had built up an intolerable heat, and

---

50 Goose and gander: during that memorable year teaching in France my French friends seized every opportunity to remind me that my countrymen had burned Joan of Arc.

I had decided I preferred to be sodden rather than steamed. The only private hostel was full; the municipal *albergue* had space, but was cramped and poorly equipped. Bleagh.

It had been a long stage: not particularly steep, but drab, soggy, and hard work; by 6.00 p.m. the dormitory was full of sleeping bodies.

Although the hostel was pretty crummy, it was open, and the sparse facilities were to a large degree tolerable given the warmth of the hosts: a Dutch couple full of good cheer and fluent in English. I settled myself into my narrow space, showered, washed my wet clothes, stuffed them into the dryer, and looked around for company.

Which materialized in the form of Jacques and Carrine, who had been walking together. Carrine, a shy lass from Switzerland, had started from Geneva; Jacques had started (like Nicole) in Le Puy. I had met them both, briefly, in previous days. Carrine was in her early thirties, Jacques in his sixties: he had retired on 15 August and started walking on the 19th: it was now 1 October. What a brilliant way to start your retirement.

The thing you immediately noticed about Jacques was that his left arm was missing, cropped off at the elbow. Although over the next few days I would spend hours chatting with him I never mustered the courage to ask him why. Despite the many demands of the Way, he coped admirably, only asking for help first thing in the morning to tie his boot laces. He had a very individual gait as he walked, swinging wide his staff with every pace.

Now the two of them welcomed my suggestion that we find a café and a bite to eat. Our hosts willingly recommended a hostelry, which after a search through the dusky streets of the little town turned out to be a tiny restaurant run by a family. The mother served us, pleased that we had been sent her way: indeed, her cooking was excellent.

It proved to be one of the most agreeable meals of the entire Camino. Jacques was wonderfully convivial, full of cheerful humour; and Carrine, flanked as she was by two old codgers intent on enjoying themselves, lost her reserve and, with the help of a glass of Rioja, was soon chattering merrily.

A vivid memory stands out from the conversation: Jacques expounding upon a delicacy he had discovered in a tapas bar in Logroño, which he termed *le grouin*. Upon enquiry this turned out to be sliced and grilled pig's snout. *Le grouin* – say it nasally, with enthusiasm – completely tickled my fancy, a splendidly onomatopoeic word.

Nájera – Navarre – is a small town, barely 7,000 strong. In the eleventh and twelfth centuries it was the capital of the Kingdom of Navarre. I found it a daunting thought: today the little community is scarcely bustling.

> **Golden lads and girls all must,**
> **As chimney-sweepers, come to dust.**[51]

In a more sombre mood – I had communicated the thought to my companions – we wandered back to the hostel.

---

51 *Cymbeline* Act IV, Scene II.

Nájera – Cirueña – Santo Domingo de la Calzada

Day 10

The road was penetrating more deserted territory.

Just outside Nájera you pass a pelota court (how pleasing to discover that this very regional game is so actively played), and then the path winds steeply upwards through a region of protected forest, the wide red earth track bisecting the groves of pines. A steep little climb, it tested the pilgrim's roadworthiness, presaging a short journey but a wearying day. Although I would reach that night's accommodation barely six hours later, I would fall asleep fully clothed, scarcely remembering to remove my boots.

Much of the day's walking would prove unremarkable, through remote and featureless farmland. Although we were still some days away from the Meseta, the high plain of central Spain, I was starting to get accustomed to dullness.

The stand-out element from the journey that day was the village of Cirueña. I was becoming aware that parts of Spain

114

seemed devoid of Spaniards, and Cirueña was a striking example. Just inside the village boundary the path led past the entrance to a smart new golf complex. Outside stood a trio of expensive shiny automobiles. Then came the first of a series of attractively built, modern, carefully maintained houses, accompanied by a well-equipped playground.

Street after street, all unoccupied.

The locals call it *Se Vende*: For Sale.

As a piece of speculative building – and Spain seems to have made this something of a national sport – I have never seen anything to match it. In 2002 Jane and I had taken a winter break on the Costa del Sol, and from our window counted twelve cranes, all busy. A decade later here was the result. The wasted investment, the useless effort, the level of debt: eye-watering, and economically paralysing.

A miasma – not of death, precisely, but of life stillborn – lay over *Se Vende*. It should have rung with children playing, but nothing moved, except spooked pilgrims hastening through, relieved to rejoin the main road shortly before Santo Domingo and get back to a degree of traffic and noise.

The place was eerie: Spain, after the virus. It felt as if we were walking through a film set. Cirueña sat marooned out in the countryside, miles from any major centre, devoid of employment, focus, infrastructure, any reason to exist. The whole region is short of people: a graph of the area shows the sparse local population fell by more than two-thirds between 1950 and 2000, a picture that would be repeated right across rural northern Spain (and, Nicole had assured me, much of southern France).

You cannot blame the regional council for sanctioning such development in the hope of drawing the people back.

But they were pushing against a potent economic tide, as young people were drawn away to new opportunities in the major cities.

The true irony about Cirueña was that it had only just been built. In the days ahead, the Way would pass through two villages – long-established, thousand-year-old villages – with a resident population of one. In the end I stopped photographing yet another house which had collapsed as its roof timbers gave way. It became commonplace to walk through towns and see not a single soul. Only in the cities did I spot any children, and in fact most of Spain's population is concentrated around Madrid and the coastal fringe. Spain's birth rate is lower than the European average, as is its population density. Coming from teeming Britain, where inward migration is a national anxiety, and successive governments are berated over the housing shortage, to walk through deserted northern Spain felt very, very odd.

A day or so later I walked for a morning with a trilingual Catalonian pilgrim from Barcelona, who told me Spain has over a million unoccupied houses.[52]

The Camino itself lifts this bleak picture, a river of life running through an arid land. I came across a number of recently established *albergues*, and heard stories of grandsons or granddaughters returning to their ancestral home to help their grandparents run the family café. Pilgrims may be famously parsimonious, but they need to eat and sleep.

---

52 He was way off the mark. According to *The Guardian* (23 February 2014) there are over 3.4 million unoccupied houses in Spain, out of a European total exceeding 11 million. Even in the UK there are more than 700,000. The same article reported more than 4 million homeless in Europe.

My favourite form of mind candy, science fiction, is fascinated by the collapse of civilization, to the extent that it has become an enduring meme. From a green perspective I fairly frequently grow sick of the human race and its criminal abuse of our small blue planet. You can make a good case for seeing humanity as a plague for which Gaia will hopefully soon find a cure. I acknowledge that this train of thought sits very uneasily with my equally strongly held Christian convictions about the value of humankind, redeemed at incalculable cost, and the love of the Creator who saw that what He had made was good.

Yet walking the Camino, through terrain suggesting what such a post-apocalyptic world might look like, left me aware that my frequent misanthropy is not well rooted. As little as half a century ago, rural Spain was a productive, bustling land, supporting succeeding generations with their own traditions and language. It felt sad, and beyond sad, to see it thus withered.

The Albergue Casa del Santo in Santo Domingo de la Calzada provided me a roof and a bed. I dozed the afternoon away, emerging at dusk to visit the town's cathedral and attend mass, well supported by the cohort of pilgrims. The *albergue*'s garden houses the chickens that take their fortnightly turns in the cathedral precincts, their coop actually installed in the building itself.

The chickens pay tribute to the miracle of the cock. There are minor variants, but these are the basics. It all happened, of course, Long Ago:

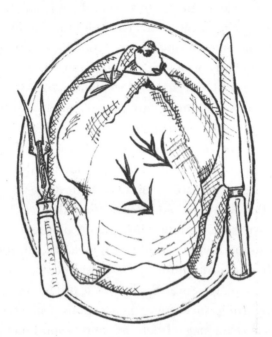

A pilgrim couple, accompanied by their teenage son, stayed overnight in the town. The lad caught the eye of the innkeeper's sultry daughter but, modest and devout, the young man did not respond to her advances. Slighted, she hid a silver cup in his pack, then raised the alarm after he and his parents had departed the following morning.

The local constabulary, or their medieval counterparts, pursued the boy, arrested, tried, and swiftly hanged him, while his parents continued oblivious to Santiago. Yet – *mirabile dictu* – he did not die, but persisted, dangling on the gallows, until his parents returned. Discovering what had happened, the distraught couple intruded upon the sheriff at lunch, just as he was about to carve his roast chicken. "Rubbish!" he cried, having heard their strange tale. "If that boy is alive then my chicken will come to life and leap from its dish." At this point the chicken... well, you can guess the rest. The lad was released from his long ordeal, the girl was arraigned in his stead, and the reunited family returned home. Legend does not relate what became of the bird, but centuries later its relatives – perhaps its descendants – still grace the cathedral.

The trained editorial eye asks questions at this point. Why were the parents so dozy? How come no one informed the sheriff that his lynchee yet lived? Such pedantry: this is Myth.

Many pilgrims seemed to be suffering that night, and one young woman had a nasty infection in her foot. Through no foresight or merit of my own, I was faring better than most.

A more trivial matter occupied my forebrain. I had left both comb and razor in Hastings, and my increasing hairiness was rendering me daily more squalid. For several years I had resorted to a buzz cut, in tacit acknowledgment that nature's bounty was growing sparse. Now, to be blunt, I required a comb. Not that there were many mirrors on the Camino, but I had difficulty recognizing the scruffy vagabond in the occasional shop window. Surely, I admonished myself, a pilgrim should be occupied with higher matters?

The comb made me feel a lot better. The facial shrubbery remained.

Santo Domingo – Belorado
Day 11

s a rule the Camino Frances threads its way through rural Spain, and cars can be rare.

Not so today. The route from Santo Domingo to Belorado follows closely the N-120 (or, more probably, the trunk road tracks the old pilgrim way); consequently, that day's journey was accompanied by noise and traffic fumes. With the constant road improvements the trusty yellow waymarks can easily be lost or obscured, and the inattentive pilgrim may find himself trudging along the highway. That day's travel would be undertaken in the open, rain or shine. A thirsty, unforgiving day.

I hoisted my pack that morning wearily. The next three days, to Burgos, looked like hard work, both steep and bleak. I was now eleven days into my journey, and though I did not know it, the toughest stretch lay ahead. It was ceasing to be exceptional that I would spend a day putting one foot ahead of the other, scanning unfamiliar landscapes, spending hours alone. The nuances and complexity of my life at home were fading from my immediate memory, and day by day I was constructing a fresh identity – that of pilgrim. But before that could truly take root I had some internal landscapes to traverse.

Just outside the village of Grañón, the Way crosses yet another of Spain's many internal borders, this time into Castilla y León. This is a region with three names, rarely a good sign: Castilla y León (Spanish); Castiella y Llión (Leonese); Castela e León (Galician). Formally created in 1983, it has its own coat of arms, flag, and regional government. An anthem has been proposed, but none as yet adopted, which speaks for itself.

The uneasy conjoining of Castilla and Leon first took place in 1230, but nearly eight hundred years later it is still not a region in harmony. Political graffiti occupy every bridge and outbuilding in Spain, but now their distribution picked up sharply, and it was easy to grasp the import of daubed slogans and defaced signboards calling for the re-creation of autonomous León.[53]

Pau, my Catalan friend from Barcelona, compared the country to a badly made cake.

The combined principality is vast, the third largest autonomous region of Europe, but with a population of just 2.5 million. It contains the sublime (or, to the less mystical, acutely boring) Meseta, the high plateau of the Iberian peninsula.

If I had thought a little harder, I would have realized: the Vortex is, above all, dull.

---

53 The volume of graffiti surpasses that of any London railway siding, and right across Spain I found myself questioning the drive to universal literacy. However, the Spanish are not entirely to blame. The day before two Dutch blokes had whizzed past on their bikes. Five minutes later I caught up with them, one resignedly holding both machines while the other added his comments in felt tip to the foot of an historic plinth.

As the name implies, Castilla is derived from the region's many castles. Until the discovery of the tomb of St James, the peninsula was largely under the control of the Moors. A thousand years later the place names and the ruins of these castles bear testimony to the bloody centuries before the long Moorish mastery came to an end.

In Burgos I would encounter this history first hand, but now the day was given over to plodding. An hour or so outside of Belorado the road passed through Viloria de Rioja, a tiny village notable as the birthplace of Santo Domingo de la Calzada, St Dominic of the Causeway, the talented engineer who did so much to improve the pilgrim experience. Born in 1019, St Dominic was responsible for bridging the Rio Oja and for constructing the principal route between Nájera and Redecilla del Camino, and is consequently patron saint of the Spanish Civil Engineers.

The baptismal font where St Dominic was christened is preserved in the local church, but with a robust disregard for history and sentiment the house where he was born has been demolished.

It was not a day for dawdling, given the traffic fumes, and by 1.00 p.m. I had reached Belorado and the Albergue Cuatro Cantones, a kindly private hostel with an enclosed swimming pool in the back garden. I washed my clothes and showered, luxuriating in the abundant hot water. When I emerged to explore, Belorado was in siesta mode, the streets deserted apart from stray pilgrims. I hoicked out my camera and took my time fossicking around the shabby ancient town, especially admiring the church bell tower, lavishly decorated with storks' nests. Above the tower, wheeling high in the deep blue, I could see several vast birds: they didn't look like vultures, and we were well south of the Pyrenees. Carrine (whom I met on the church steps) assured me they were eagles.

I returned to the *albergue* garden, which echoed to a quintet of Spanish lads who had discovered the swimming pool, caught up on my reading in Pen's *Wilderness Within You*, and admired an ensemble of hens and rabbits, happily intermingled, in the adjoining paddock. Then, checking on my washing, which I had strung up to dry on a balcony, I discovered to my consternation that my underwear and socks were missing.

Who could possibly nick another pilgrim's underpants?

Looking askance at my fellow travellers, none of whom seemed obviously perverted, I scanned the nearby rooftops – it was a windy day, and a hunky Japanese guy had lost his tartan shorts an hour or so before (they were draped prettily across a nearby chimney, quite inaccessible). But I had used safety pins to attach my clothing to the line; the rest of my garments were still present and correct. If it came to it, I could go commando, but the loss of my socks was more irritating. My pared-to-simplicity packing had not allowed for errant clothing. (The sock routine was one pair dry, one pair drying, one pair in service – pilgrims and other long-distance hobblers can be easily discerned by the socks flapping from their packs.)

Irritated and bemused, I set the matter to one side and went forth in search of nourishment. By now the town had emerged from its bedrooms and the local *supermercado* was open: a real treasure trove of regional food and wine. In its aisles I met the tall American whose comment about Nicole had caused me such heart-searching. She greeted me cheerfully, introduced herself as Goldhara, and called across to her sister Jan – the family resemblance unmistakable, both slender, positive, rangy blondes of middle years. The two of them were on the same mission, so we combined forces and returned to the hostel laden with bottles, chorizo, cheese, and bread. Of such inconsequential invitations are friendships made.

My Swiss army knife uncorked the wine and sliced the sausage. Out in the garden we settled for a chat. Over the course of the next hour or so I learned that Goldhara oscillated between New Mexico and California, a difference in elevation of 7,000 feet, depending on the season; that both of them – but Goldhara in particular – enjoyed extreme sports, notably off-road mountain biking and white water rafting with her husband Dennis; that the previous year she and Jan had walked the stretch of Camino between Le Puy and St Jean, and this year planned to press through to Finisterre; that both of them took the idea of pilgrimage very seriously, but (the consequence of a strict upbringing) had little time or respect for the Christian faith; and that they loved their wine and knew a good deal about it. "We're the Wine Sisters," added Jan, happily. And so they were. Kindly, forthright, curious, droll, they would prove excellent companions.

That night, as we were heading upstairs, to my surprise I ran into Nicole: I had not realized she was staying at the same hostel. I greeted her, rather awkwardly, and she grinned back. "Did you find your clothes?" she asked. "They were dry, so I took them down and hid them under your sleeping bag, so no one would steal them."

Belorado – San Juan de Ortega – Agés – Burgos

Days 12 and 13

The following morning I gloomily examined Brierley's profile map showing the day's climb: an accrued ascent of 500 metres, which Brierley helpfully multiplies by five to indicate the equivalent on the flat, and by implication the wear and tear to knees and spirit. The journey would be challenging and long – over 16 miles in real money. There was one compensation: most of the route followed paths and earthen tracks rather than tarmacked sterility.

I was heading for San Juan de Ortega, a remote pilgrim village with a single *albergue*. My twelfth day on the road, and I was starting to feel, cautiously, as if I could do this thing.

My knees had begun to click, slightly alarmingly. There was nothing to be done, so I ignored them.

The day's route wound through a series of small villages, Tosantos and Villambistia and Espinosa and Villafranca, each largely and eerily deserted. Before the road really started to climb I stopped for a coffee in Villafranca Montes de Oca. There are several "Villafrancas" on the Camino, towns possibly created and certainly colonized by Franks (Rhineland Germans and northern French) who passed through as pilgrims and returned to work and live. Seated in the foothills of a wild upland area much haunted by bands of bandits, the village welcomed pilgrims as early as the ninth century. The bandits thoroughly approved, one suspects.

A grim past, and a dark recent past too. After Villafranca the road climbs in earnest, winding through ancient forests of oak and pine, and on the descent you come to a memorial, the *Monumento a los Caídos*, or Monument to the Fallen. This stark affair, a block of concrete on a severe plinth, commemorates the many, many men from Burgos, 22 miles away, who were abducted, killed, and dumped here by the Fascists in the summer of 1936, during the course of the Spanish Civil War – in many ways a rehearsal for the far wider conflict then brewing.

The local authorities had set up picnic tables nearby. At first it seemed a desecration, but evidently many families climb up the long mountainside to eat, drink, and remember Uncle Miguel: all part of Spain's prolonged and unresolved effort to come to terms with its many internal divisions.

Unvarying forest is almost as tedious as unvarying fields, and I was pleased to win through to San Juan. It is a notably remote little hamlet, with a population of twenty. San Juan himself was a disciple of Santo Domingo, and like his mentor exercised his faith in a most practical way, building bridges and hospitals right through the area. Perhaps we should canonize more civil engineers? In this forgotten spot he founded an Augustinian monastery in 1150, which must have presented a welcome relief for hard-pressed pilgrims conscious of the area's murderous reputation; one can imagine men and women scurrying for its shelter as the sun sank behind the wooded hills and the bandits hammered extra nails into their cudgels. No wonder my predecessors travelled together.

San Juan is a classic pilgrim halt, but it was barely 2.00 p.m., the *albergue* was described as basic and draughty, and the tiny settlement offered one small café and the prospect of an empty evening. Consulting my map I saw that a few miles further on lay the altogether busier (if still tiny) village of Agés, with a choice of hostels.

At the little café in San Juan I ran into a crowd of familiar faces: my Irish friends Brian, Patrick, and Bríd, and – sitting by herself – Nicole. I greeted my Celtic cousins, and introduced Nicole. Off we trooped together, and just as we entered Agés we overtook Theodore, a genial American, of whom more anon. The Albergue San Rafael lay at the entrance to the village, and there we stopped.

The *albergue* was a mother-and-son affair, clean and tidy enough, but definitely on the cramped side: the six of us ended up stacked in bunks in a small triangular room, with one windowless bathroom whose light only came on once you had locked the door (it took some while to discover this).

The village provided very little other than a bar (though the following morning we would find a small but well-stocked grocery store offering croissants and excellent coffee). But our *albergue* boasted a modest restaurant, and here Theodore came into his own.

I had first encountered Theodore a couple of days before, when I had passed him on the road. With his cherubic ageless face and distinctive headgear (a straw boater from which he had removed the crown) he cut a memorable figure. He was having a hard time of it, suffering not only from agonizing shin splints but also from evil blisters. I had treated his feet with iodine, and on discovering that he lacked inner socks had given him a pair (which was why the incident of the washing line had so narked me). Despite his considerable discomfort he was never less than cheerful, his courage and good humour making him an agreeable companion. I travelled with him on and off for days afterwards, leaving him behind early in the morning and greeting him late in the afternoon as he limped in, face set but a grin always to hand. I learned later that he too had served in the Marines.

The restaurant, like the rest of the establishment, promised little and successfully delivered it. But our hostess, the lady of the house, was a generously built and wonderfully sympathetic woman, full of fun and refusing to let the complete lack of a common language spoil the evening. We responded in kind and she clowned her way through the meal, insisting that everyone finish their portions and bestowing a kiss on those who obliged – notably Theodore, whose impish demeanour invited mischief and whose bald pate was glowing with *señora*'s approval by the end of the evening.

It had been a long, drab day.

That night the company slept soundly, dead to the world, nine hours apiece, rousing late to stumble to the wayside café I had spotted the previous evening, and a place on its upturned barrels. Here wonderfully fragrant almond croissants and deep cups of aromatic coffee set us on our feet.

In the crowded store I ran into Alain, my Hemingway enthusiast, who recommended the local speciality: black pudding made with rice. I kept my eyes open, but it did not appear on any subsequent menu.

Outside we shrugged our way into our packs, and I bade farewell to Brian (who was short on time, and was planning to catch a bus) and to Patrick, Nicole, and Bríd, who were far swifter; and to Theodore, who was far slower.

This is the nature of pilgrimage: you may never meet again, so you drop your guard and allow a true rapport to develop. They were good companions all. Weeks later at Stansted Airport, waiting in the passport queue on my way home, I met a girl I had never seen before. "The Irish guys – Brian and that – they told me, if I saw you, to say they had been pleased to walk with you, and to wish you well."

An hour brought me to the village of Atapuerca, whose caves were designated a UNESCO World Heritage Site in 2000. The caverns of Atapuerca, discovered when a mining company was cutting a rail link to the mines nearby, have generated intense interest because of the antiquity of human traces found there, the oldest in Europe. The deposits range from early stone tools and hominid remains dating back at least 900,000 years, right through to evidence of Neolithic and Bronze Age occupation.

Archaeology has always fascinated me. I can remember, as a child, presenting a curious flake of flint to a neighbour, a keen amateur archaeologist. She examined it seriously, turning it to catch the light, then passed it back to me. "Yes, it has definitely been worked," she told me. "Keep it carefully."

I did as she bade me, storing the fragment properly annotated in a glass-topped display drawer of my father's imposing black Chinese cabinet (mainly housing his own childhood collection of butterflies and moths). It sat there alongside a fossilized hippo's tooth and a small votary figurine, thousands of years old, still bearing traces of light blue glaze, which my father had picked up in Cairo during the Second World War – a purchase that today might have landed both him and the vendor in trouble. (My father was a captain in the Royal Artillery, and, possessing a degree in French and Spanish, became a liaison officer between the British Army and the Free French forces in the area. A talented linguist, he had soon mastered street Arabic, and used to reckon that in the markets of Cairo he could get down to the French price – goods came in four prices: the American, the British, the French, and the Arabic. As a child I cherished the little figure, imagining my father's bold negotiations.)

My good-natured neighbour came to regret her advice, I suspect: on many mornings over that summer her breakfast peace would be broken by a small boy on her doorstep, proffering an interesting stone.

Just outside the village of Atapuerca there was a visitor centre with rather basic information, and it was possible to visit the site, where digging still continues. This felt like too much the tourist; as I had another long day ahead, I turned away from temptation.

There is something about the Camino that compels you not to dawdle. You are not on holiday; you are not a sightseer. The open road drags at your mind: it is what you do, what you are. You do not have to be a flagellant, but neither may you doss around. You start to develop a vocabulary of obligation, inventing excuses to carry on, always avoiding the truth: that a compulsion grips you.

It is this, I think, which lies behind the barely concealed scorn the long-distance pilgrim may evince for those who ship their luggage ahead (there are many such services), or who walk a week at a time. They are not of our number. They have not earned their blisters. Once the call of the Way has entered your soul, it sets you apart. You know in your marrow that only those who have trudged the distance beneath their pack can completely understand. You are a pilgrim, in weather fair or foul. Buffeted or baked, vulnerable but enduring, you walk on.

And yet there is a tension. You are yourself the enemy. Your challenges may ostensibly be those of the road, but the greater challenges lie within: your weakness, your fear, your self-doubt. St James confers this gift, that you learn a measure of self-mastery.

One of the more notable qualities of the Camino is that it shows you the unlovely underbelly of Spain, the bits no tourist will see.

So it was with the approaches to Burgos. Burgos is one of the jewels of the Camino, a city of art and culture. As with all human settlements, it has its grimy side, and the trudge that day through the industrial zone to the east of the city was one I would have gladly avoided. The recommended route skirted Burgos airfield, notable for its stern security signs – beyond my romper suit Spanish, but one got the gist – every few hundred metres along its interminable chain-link fence. The trackside litter, a hazard right across Spain, had been blown against the fence in disagreeable profusion, and I tramped through plastic, paper, cans, and cartons. Such limitless trash abraded the spirit. To the landscape, and probably to its people, we ephemeral pilgrims had little greater consequence: flotsam, blown by the gusts of history.

My dour mood lifted when, quite abruptly, the route emerged from the industrial zone, crossed the cheerful Rio Arlanzón, and entered a delightful riverside park running right into the centre of the city. What a relief, after the concrete and aluminium and rusty steel of the previous kilometres, to find myself walking through hip-high grass; a tight knot of unhappiness relaxed as I relished the shade trees and savoured the river-scented air.

After an hour or so a fresh worry intruded on my mind: I could not go very far wrong by following the course of the river, which led all the way into the heart of the city, but this felt all too much like a stroll in the country, and signposts were scarce. My shoulders ached, my feet were expressing their opinion, and I could not locate this parkland on my map (I later realized that the large-scale map only showed the very centre of Burgos). I approached several picnicking families whose English was as fluent as my Castilian, on each occasion retreating with apologies and a strong suspicion that I had not improved the cause of international relations.

Gradually the city centre hove into view. A low wall ran along the river, bordered by a metalled path, with the measurements marked off in units of 100 metres (not a source of joy, when hobbling slowly and painfully). Along the path bounded the eager young, exulting in their strength and lightness, bouncing past my ancient grubbiness.

At a wayside stone bench I eased off my pack and leaned against it for twenty minutes or so, eyes closed, until my throbbing frame had ceased to pulse so unpleasantly. Then I fished out Brierley and inspected my options. Most of the *albergues* required the traveller to delve into the city centre, and this failed to appeal. Off to the left, however, on the same side of the river, stood Emmaus House, Casa de Peregrinos Emaús, "with shared meal following the tradition of Emmaus with Christian prayer and blessing". One suspects Brierley of quoting from a translated website. Linguistic deficiencies aside, this sounded just the ticket.

By this point I was alert to the nuances between the municipal hostels, the privately run alternatives, and the occasional religious houses. The municipal establishments are often vast affairs, basic, sparsely equipped; the private hostels are less predictable, but generally more comfortable and slightly more expensive; the religious houses – where they occur – are consistently cheerful and compassionate.

But I couldn't find this one. A frustrating hour later,

slogging up and down the outskirts of Burgos and attracting amused glances from the natives, I unhitched my pack again. I had spoken to shopkeepers and passers-by; I had been laughed at by school kids, and old grannies had shaken their heads at my faltering questions. It was siesta time, and the streets were emptying.

With ebbing confidence I approached a middle-aged, rotund gentleman ambulating gently down the street.

"Emaús? Si."

He nodded cheerfully, turned smartly about and headed back the way he had come, leading me several hundred metres up a side street and round to the back of an imposing Catholic church. There, in the shadow of a large tree, quite invisible from the road, stood a door. "Emaús," gestured my saviour proudly. He mimed pressing a bell, beamed, and resumed his afternoon constitutional. A good guide, who went the extra mile.[54]

I pressed the bell, and waited. After a worrying silence the door was unlatched and a little bent grey-haired woman blinked up at me. In response to my stammered enquiry she nodded and held the door open. "Put the boots here," she told me crisply in French-tinged English, and gestured to an entirely empty rack. "Follow me."

In my stockinged feet I padded after her over the marble floor and up a sweeping stone staircase, then another. Portraits and busts of assorted divines stared disapprovingly down, and I felt like some slovenly burglar invading a stately home. The guide book had mentioned that the church stood adjacent

---

54 I subsequently discovered that the hostel had relocated a year or two before – just about the only significant inaccuracy I found in Brierley's valuable guide.

to a Jesuit college, and slightly overawed I compensated by imagining the august sculpted empty spaces thronged with boisterous juvenile priests. At the top the elderly lady paused while I caught my breath, then ushered me into a dining room with reassuringly commonplace melamine refectory tables. Here she took my details, stamped my *credencial*, and looked at my weary features with compassion. Leading me down a corridor, she pushed open a door to a small room holding three double bunks. "Don't put your pack on the beds," she instructed. "Showers are over there. There is plenty of hot water," she added significantly. "You will feel like a new man."

After the long hard day her severe kindness was a balm to the spirit. I stripped and stood for long minutes under the powerful jet, allowing the cares and aches and frustrations to sluice away. For a night, I had found a refuge.

Feeling brighter I wandered back into the refectory and there found Cristiane, my host, going over her papers, and ventured to ask for her story. She had lived for thirty years in New York, but when her American husband died she returned to her native France, and now spent a good part of each year helping out on the Camino. "I am just here for another week," she confided. "Then I will walk the Camino Primitivo."

I looked at her tiny ancient form with some astonishment: the Camino Primitivo is famously demanding and not for the faint-hearted. She lifted her chin. "I have done it before," she added, slightly truculently. In Santiago I would meet her again, climbing steadily up a long steep slope, setting a good pace. She greeted me with delight, mingled with pride: she had just completed her pilgrimage.

On the road a few days previously I had met a rather splendid voluble hippyish pilgrim, a lithe and profusely hairy Frenchman in his thirties, retracing his steps from Santiago towards his native land. We had stopped to chat, and I learned that he was a stonemason, navigating his way from one architectural prodigy to another. He expanded for several minutes on the traceries of stone to be viewed in the Catedral de Santa Maria, in Burgos.

With this in mind I left my washing slung across the tiny balcony and ambled again down the long stone staircases, rejoicing as every evening at my lightweight feet. Cristiane told me to be back at 7.30 for the evening meal, so I had time to view all the monuments I wanted.

Except that I didn't want. Discovering at the entrance to the cathedral that I had left my *credencial* behind (it would have afforded a discount off the substantial entry fee) I was seized with a sudden anomie, and turned away instead to wander round the outside. An astonishing confection, Burgos Cathedral is vast. It took me ten minutes to circumnavigate it. I promised myself I would return.

As I reached the main square I found myself jostled to the side of the road by juvenile Crusaders.

Burgos is the birthplace of Count Rodrigo Díaz de Vivar, better known as El Cid (The Lord), a Muslim term of respect. El Cid (c. 1043–99) was a military commander, pugnacious soldier of fortune, and tactician of considerable ability, who at various times fought the Muslims on behalf of Castile, and for the Muslim leaders of Zaragoza against other Muslim rivals in the south. The allegiances of the period were complex and shifting, and El Cid was also victorious in battles against the Muslim rulers of Lérida and their Christian allies, as well as against a large Christian army under King Sancho Ramírez of Aragon. To think of him as a shining Christian hero leading the forces of light against the screaming Muslim hordes is quite far from the facts.

None of this mattered to the youngsters in imitation chainmail and white surplices adorned with large red crosses, who waved their swords and chased one another through the narrow streets, and posed victorious on the steps of the cathedral for the cameras of their admiring parents.

I looked on slightly nauseated. The young sword-brandishers were undoubtedly in tune with the spirit of the early medieval pilgrims, for whom the rescuing of the holy places of Jerusalem from the hands of the infidel would have seemed entirely laudable. But what on earth were their parents doing, allowing them to perpetuate these horrific enmities? Evidently the Reconciliation Walk of 1996 had sunk from memory.[55]

I wandered back down towards the Rio Arlanzón, and there discovered on its banks a boost to the spirits: a medieval fair in full swing, with merrie knights and maidens everywhere, and dozens of stalls selling jewellery, scents, chocolate, local

---

55 The Reconciliation Walk, comprised mainly of evangelical Protestants, started from Cologne, Germany, on Easter Sunday 1996, 900 years after the departure from Cologne of the First Crusade. The intention was to apologize for the atrocities committed in the name of Christ during the Crusades. Going from city to city, one team crossed France, Switzerland, Austria, Italy, Slovenia, Croatia, Montenegro, Albania, Macedonia, and Greece. A second team set out from Germany and passed through Slovakia, Hungary, and Bulgaria. The Walkers stopped at sites in Turkey, Syria, and Lebanon before entering Jerusalem on 15 July 1999, the 900th anniversary of the killing of about 60,000 residents and the destruction of the city. Over 2,000 Walkers participated, from twenty-seven countries. The Walk made repeated headlines across the region, but clearly not in Spain.

ham and honey, olives, soap, toys. I paid, nibbled, and sipped, suddenly happy, entranced by flavours and smells, surrounded by bustle and the works of ingenious hands.

With evening drawing in, I climbed back towards the main bridge over the river, past the enormous equestrian statue of El Cid in full gallop across the Puente de Santa Maria towards an unspecified foe. El Cid was inseparable from his great warhorse, Babieca, and requested that the two of them be buried together in the grounds of the monastery of San Pedro de Cardeña.

Later he was reinterred in Burgos Cathedral with his wife, Doña Jimena, but without his trusty steed, which tells you what Mrs Cid thought about the arrangement.[56]

Back at the hostel I met other pilgrims, an Italian couple and two dark Spaniards, and at Cristiane's invitation we made our way downstairs to the well-attended evening mass. Afterwards we sat down to an adequate, if frugal, meal. At the end Cristiane passed around a basket, and asked us to pay what we thought appropriate. "What you have just eaten," she explained, "was made available by the generosity of yesterday's guests. What we serve tomorrow depends on what you give now." In a spasm of sympathy I deposited several notes.

Before we retired for the night Cristiane led a brief meditation and discussion on the nature and purpose of pilgrimage, then invited each of us to take a slip of paper for the journey. Mine read: "God is not words, he is an extraordinary inner experience."

More than I would have expected, I treasured the Christian welcome at Emaús.

---

56 Babieca's tomb still stands at the monastery.

Burgos – Hornillos
Day 14

"Through the window, I watch what Jesus is watching – the pageant of passing clouds, majestic, slow, freighted with glory," writes Pen Wilcock. "The extravaganza of clouds draws my soul up out of my body, and drenches my thoughts with purity."

Pen's conversations with Jesus in *The Wilderness Within You*, often extraordinarily apposite, provided a piquant counterpoint to my early mornings. No matter how sluggish the organism, the dawn skies eased my aching shoulders and boosted my mood. One morning the sky was flooded the most improbable Barbie pink, glowing from the wayside rocks and the distant wind turbines.

Every pilgrim includes the clouds in his or her assessment of the morning. The slow procession of the skies would be my companion over the next few days, for after Burgos the Camino leaves the world of bricks and pavements, and enters what Brierley, ever the comedian, terms "the divine Meseta".

The Meseta (from *mesa*, table) comprises the central heartland of Spain. It is flat, dry, mostly deserted, and the point on my journey where for the first time I really encountered the Total Perspective Vortex.

My day's destination, Hornillos, makes the point well. The suffix *-illos* is a diminutive (in this case, literally, "little oven") and can be found in place names across the Meseta (in the next few days the Camino would pass through, for example, Terradillos de Templarios and Calzadilla de los Hermanillos). This sense of insignificance accords easily with the sheer vastness of the plain: the pilgrim is indeed diminished, a momentary blip, and there is little to do but watch clouds and navigate the inner landscape.

I am comfortable with my own company. Solitary in youth, the only child of elderly parents, I find my greatest peace in the lonely pursuits – fishing, reading, running, carpentry, gardening, golf. (If your slice matches mine, a golf course is solitude incarnate. I became a member of the FODR[57] many years ago.)

Paradoxically, my closest friends have usually been members of large tribes. Marrying Pen brought me the added bonus of five step-daughters.

The Meseta would test my capacity for solitude to the limit. No pilgrim on the Camino is truly alone, of course, but the nearest specimen of *hom. sap.* might easily be hundreds of metres ahead or behind. Nothing to watch but the dusty brown road beneath your boots or the indifferent clouds above; not a bird, not a rat; barely a bush – just the utterly uniform sunflowers, and, once, on the horizon a vast harvester, rendered minuscule by distance.

---

57 Friends of the Deep Rough

It would prove the toughest part of the Way.

The Meseta set in train a sequence of thoughts that would occupy me for several days. Basically, they revolved around the women I have known. I don't think I am of unusually ardent temper, but I enjoy, respect, and appreciate female company, and value the finely nuanced interchanges that are part of conversation between men and women.

The consequence is that from my mid-teens I have had many female friends, and in my youth a generous number of girlfriends, as well as two wives. I say this not with any sense of cutting notches in a stick: it is not a question of pride.

The fall-out from these connections now occupied my thoughts. Long-buried incidents forced their way back to the surface. Sad or furious partings returned with awful freshness. It came to me that I had left, over the course of my life, a string of wounded, disappointed women in my wake: not that I had loved and tossed aside, but rather that I had failed to live up to expectations. In seeking to be kind I had raised hopes; in failing to guard my boundaries I had misled. I thought again of the days walking with Nicole, and winced.

Over the next days the Way proved pitiless. Conversation after conversation, occasion by occasion, the ladies of my life lined up to remind me of the times when I had promised more than I could deliver, or had demanded more than I had any right to expect. I recalled letters full of pain and bitterness, and my stumbling, inadequate replies; telephone calls where I held the receiver for minutes on end, listening to someone sobbing, utterly unable to do more than to acknowledge that I had messed up yet again, inexcusably forgotten an important occasion, simply failed in my duty of kindness or care, betrayed a trust.

One afternoon, many years ago, I was sitting reading a book when the phone rang. "Tony, you toad," accused a cross young Australian voice, "you've forgotten you were picking me up." I had.

The worst of it was, I could not make amends. I could not go back; could not resurrect old friendships, track down old flames. I had no coin sufficient for the task. To attempt to do so would offend, upset, and mislead afresh. There was no salve I could offer. No apology would suffice: the women in question would be embarrassed and irritated to hear from me.

The ending of my first marriage came when I concluded, with a most heavy heart, that Jane would be better off without me. Her palpable unhappiness was intertwined with my presence. "My heart sinks when I hear your car in the drive," she told me one wretched afternoon. I had reached the end of my resources, and they were insufficient.

To dwell thus on the shabbiness of the past can become self-indulgent, egotistical: who are you, that they should care? The need to atone added another voice to the litany of guilt.

After a few days of this unwilling introspection I realized that the parade of accusations was starting to generate its own false consolation. If you are only fit to be wiped from the bottom of another's shoe, you know your place. But this is a lie.

> Soul, self; come, poor Jackself, I do advise
> You, jaded, let be; call off thoughts awhile
> Elsewhere; leave comfort root-room.[58]

---

58   Gerard Manley Hopkins:"My own heart let me more have pity on"

I started to draw comfort from the flat, calm, open spaces around me, and the utter simplicity of dead dark sunflowers, stretching to the limit of vision under the bright October skies. The Meseta had exposed me to the cold wind, but now it was offering such succour as it could.

I have been a Christian for several decades, and in that period I have sung hymns without number on the topics of sin and guilt and redemption. I understand the doctrine, but until I walked the Meseta I did not truly get it for myself: the inescapable burden, the ineradicable stain.

Yet this is not the whole picture, of course.

As I walked on, I started to pray in tongues. It is a gift I received many years ago, and it has been a constant solace. "We do not know what to pray for as we ought, but the Spirit himself intercedes for us with groanings too deep for words."[59] I might not be able to make amends, but I knew a Friend who could. Whatever my opinion on the conduct and morals of A. Collins, bloke, mine was not the one that counted.

"This seemingly insubstantial fact revolutionised my life," wrote Adrian Plass, author of *The Sacred Diary of Adrian Plass Aged 37 ¾*. "I became a Christian when I was sixteen years old, but it wasn't until I was thirty-seven that I absorbed an essential truth. God is nice, and he likes me."

After that scarifying day it was a relief to arrive in Hornillos (population seventy). The hostel I had selected was full (the second and last occasion on which this happened), so I followed the signs through the small central square and up past the church, which dominated the little settlement, to the barely adequate Albergue Municipal.

---

59 Romans 8:26, ESV

This consisted of several modest rooms utterly crammed with bunks. There was no one in attendance, but an elderly Dutchman unlacing his boots pointed across the road. "Look in the bar," he advised, and his counsel proved sound: our host – a plump, morose individual with a heavy beard – ran both establishments.

Hornillos was no teeming metropolis. The tiny settlement had one small shop, and a bar whose menu failed to appetize. However, the square featured a couple of tables with attendant chairs. Two of these were occupied by Goldhara and Jan, the Wine Sisters, who beckoned me over and filled my glass to the brim. A convivial hour later we migrated across the square to the wall of the church, rising high above the surrounding plain in the rays of the setting sun. There we were joined by several other pilgrims, notably Mack and Jim. Having acquired bread, sausage, olives, and further vino we settled in for an evening of yarns.

Mack and Jim. Both were in their fifties, both ex-Marines,[60] strongly individual, friends since Army days. Mack was a successful realtor in Hawaii – after years of wandering the States he had met a guy in a bar, years previously, who asked him to look after a flock of goats on the island, and he had ended up staying.[61] Jim was a high-end computer technician working in health care. Sharp-witted and very fit, they made a memorable pair.

The two of them were full of extraordinary stories, particularly concerning the floods in Colorado a few weeks previously. Jim had had to abandon his brand-new,

---

60 *Pax vobiscum.* Marines no longer on active service.

61 He has since started a new company, Camino Properties.

highly prized Ford Focus (ordered from Britain – a model not commonly available in the US) to the rapidly rising floodwaters, after a very uncomfortable period sitting on the roof: a state-of-the art fire truck had rescued him, only to be trapped in turn. Mack, who had planned to join him for the trip out to Spain, was turned away by federal officials miles from Jim's house, and elected to make his way across country, up and over the intervening ridge. Because of their past training they were co-opted by the rescue services, and ended up working for days on end to save families from the raging waters. "We never did find my car," concluded Jim.

As I sat down next to Goldhara, she leaned towards me. "Look at Mack's left thumb," she murmured. I did, surreptitiously: the digit in question was enormous, crooked, mesmerizing. "It's his left big toe," she explained, pleased with the effect of her revelation. Jim told me a few days later that Mack had been on active duty in the British Virgin Islands when someone in a bar had objected to his interest in a young lady and had emphasized his point with a machete. By the time Mack reached a hospital the surgeons had been unable to reattach the thumb, but had found an inventive alternative. "He walked around for weeks with his hand down his trousers, plugged into his femoral artery, until the graft took," said Jim. Mack may have been short a big toe, but it didn't slow him in the slightest.[62]

The five of us drank wine and told stories until the sun sank below the distant hills and a chill settled over the square. Then we sought our bunks.

---

62 This story is not entirely true, Mack informed me later. "You don't want to know the real one," he added.

Before setting out on my travels I had purchased an inner sleeping bag of silk, impregnated with an anti-bedbug preparation. That night I was grateful for it: bedbugs are an unpleasant reality on the Camino, and the *albergue*'s mattresses were ancient and certainly infested. Earlier that evening I had chatted to a young French girl with neck and shoulders painfully swollen from an encounter a couple of nights previously: she had taken the drastic step of replacing bedding, pack, and every stitch of clothing. Looking at her inflamed skin I could entirely understand. Now I tucked my protective silk tight around my ears.[63]

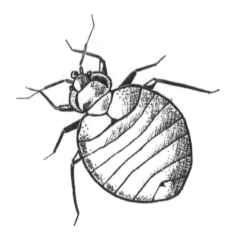

63　Bedbugs do not discriminate. There is a rather pleasing story of King John hunting in the Kingsclere area, near Basingstoke, and when the fog rolled in, his party was stranded. They sought lodging for the night at the Kingsclere tavern, where bugs so aggravated the royal person that on his return home the irritated monarch commanded a weathervane in the form of a bug be cast and placed atop the church tower. The weathervane – possibly *the* weathervane – still exists, attached to the roof of St Mary's Church.

The bugs were not the only challenge of that night. I found myself bunked beneath a corpulent moustached Frenchman who had also found the local vintage to his taste – so much so that his snores rattled the windows and kept thirty people awake. I prodded and pushed from below – at one point bracing my feet against the mattress above me and bouncing the fellow up and down. He muttered, turned over, and within seconds was sawing wood once more. I gave up.

Hornillos – Castrojeriz
Day 15

The following morning started early, thanks to my sleeping companion, and I hit the road by seven. Darkness shrouded the first kilometres, and leaving Hornillos I searched anxiously for each yellow arrow, the droplets of fog swirling around my torch beam. As I slogged up onto the open road of the Meseta I switched it off, watching the dawn penetrate the mists and gradually generate colour around me, turning greys to greens, turquoise, and amber.

By the time I reached San Bol, an isolated *albergue* nestled in the bleak, folded landscape, I looked forward to breakfast. Five euros purchased a tiny croissant and a glass of Sunny Delight, surely one of the world's most repulsive beverages. When I emerged from the little hostel the day had risen entirely.

A kilometre or so later I passed a young pilgrim sitting beside the track, spelling out on the bank a message in pebbles for following friends. He had spent the night in that deserted spot, curled in a pup tent: he was the only camping pilgrim I met.

I passed through the tiny, half-deserted villages of Hontanas and San Anton, tucked away in the crannies of the Meseta and largely ignored except by the steady stream of pilgrims. In Hontanas I investigated a niggle in my right boot which materialized as a small blister, my first. I fished out needle and Compeed, changed my socks, and continued.

San Anton features the ruins of the eleventh-century monastery and hospice of the Antonines, a French order linked to the hermit St Anthony of Egypt, and famed for its ability to cure St Anthony's Fire. The Order's symbol was the Tau (τ), the nineteenth letter of the Greek alphabet, a symbol of life or resurrection, a protection against sickness, and these days often called the "Pilgrim Cross": examples are widely on sale on the Camino.

My destination was Castrojeriz, a piece of ancient ribbon development, a larger settlement that straggles along the pilgrim route for at least two kilometres. It stands at the end of an interminable avenue of poplars stretching well over a kilometre in a die-straight line towards an isolated hill. A delightful old town, it meanders around the hillside and features several generous squares and fountains, ideal for basking in the autumn sun.

On the Calle Real (the Royal Way) I found what I was looking for, stepped into the dusky hall of the Albergue Casa Nostra, and stood blinking in the gloom. An urbane young man, tall and balding, came forward to welcome me and take my details. "You're the first today," he said in fluent English, ushering me up to the dormitories. "Take your pick." The *albergue* was a delight, spacious and accommodating, centuries old, full of exposed timber, eccentric angles, and curious modern paintings, scented with wood polish and garlic.

I showered, changed, and attended to my laundry. I was keen to explore Castrojeriz, today a sleepy place of 900 souls (enlivened briefly by a garlic festival in July), but with an impressively eventful past. The castle atop the hill was a powerful military fastness, dating back to Roman times (there is a story that the town was first founded by Julius Caesar, but remains from the Bronze Age show the location has been settled far longer). In subsequent years it was a Visigoth stronghold. During the eighth century the strategic point was fiercely contested by Muslim and Christian forces, taken and retaken several times; then, with the rise of the Camino and the local wool trade, Castrojeriz became an important municipality, before the long population drain began. At the height of the pilgrim era it boasted no fewer than eight hospitals, such as San Anton, specializing in the treatment of St Anthony's Fire.

Now its primary occupation seemed to be an extended siesta. I prowled the quiet streets savouring the worn stone and sunshine, my imagination populating its empty spaces with clanking warriors and road-weary brown-robed truth-seekers. Along one side of a leafy square stood a range of shops catering to the pilgrim trade, where I exchanged a few remarks (with the assistance of a Spanish pilgrim) with one ancient proprietor who had been running his we-sell-everything emporium for over sixty years. Some of the stock clearly dated from the previous owner. Next door stood an entirely modern hiking shop, displaying boots and walking poles. A couple of doors further down I spotted an inviting bar with tables outside, and there I stopped and chatted over an ice-cold beer with a suave elderly couple making their leisurely way westwards.

I wandered back towards the *albergue*, but was enticed by an open door with a sign reading "House of Shadows".

The House of Shadows, created by a couple of past pilgrims around the theme of friendship, is a place of respite. Signs invite travellers to sit, read, breathe awhile, help themselves to coffee. I wandered through the warren of comfortable shabby rooms. The walls are adorned with photos and abstract art, interspersed with bookshelves stuffed with books in several languages. It was a lovely location to pause for an hour or two, full of peace and beauty, and I did. One caption caught my eye:

> The purpose of words is to transmit ideas.
> When ideas are understood, words are forgotten.
> When can I find a man who has forgotten his words?
> I would really like to talk to him.

I sat for perhaps an hour, musing.

That morning I had read what Pen wrote about the importance of watching what the Father is doing, moving to that rhythm, becoming part of the heavenly dance – a dance, not a timetable.

As one consequence of my hour of peace, I finally accepted I should stop competing with the Way, and those who pass along it: stop checking my watch, racing the young and fit – or even the old and spry – stop *achieving*. A fortnight ago the same insight had come, but I'd been unable to act upon it: now, as I ended my fifteenth day on the road, it seemed within reach.

Then a bulky, untidy figure appeared in the doorway.

Eric was a computer boffin in his late thirties from Des Moines. Eager to talk, he told me that he had left his job and partner to take a year out to discover himself and find his true purpose. This led us into the foothills of psychotherapy, and since he seemed eager to expand his frame of reference I explained to him the rudiments of transactional analysis.[64] He was a fresh-faced, candid character, anxious to find his way to the truth. *My* truth, that afternoon, was that I had been enjoying the silence.

Ashamed of my inner crabbiness, I showed him another sign upstairs that had caught my attention:

On ne peut rien apprendre à un homme;
On ne peut que l'aider à trouver la réponse en lui-
même.

You can teach a man nothing;
you can only help him to find the answer within.

Eric loved this, and I left him sitting happily in the afternoon sun, reading a dog-eared copy of *I'm OK, You're OK*.[65] All well and good, but I had given in to my impatience and played

---

64 An idea developed by Canadian psychiatrist Eric Berne in the 1950s, transactional analysis is a theory of personality, which in its simplest form examines the relations, or transactions, between people. Its best known model of human behaviour uses three modes: parent / adult / child. Each of us has the capacity to relate and respond using any of these modes. Berne put forward his ideas in a seminal book, *Games People Play*.

65 *I'm OK, You're OK*, by Thomas Harris, London: Arrow Books, Random House. First published in 1968, this is an excellent introduction to transactional analysis. I had discovered TA at All Nations, with a sense of light dawning: it shines a clear beam on your own motivations, and reveals the currents behind tricky conversations.

the parent to his child. I walked away hoping I had not been overly didactic.

At the door of the House of Shadows I met the proprietor, a wonderfully eccentric, be-smocked Spaniard of middle years, painfully thin, his long hair in pigtails. He was parking his ancient pushbike, and consented to my photographing him and his steed. "My Maserati," he told me, patting the ramshackle machine affectionately.

I had walked that day alone, by choice, but back at Casa Nostra I ran into Jim and Mack, Jan and Goldhara. They had been joined by Hume, an ebullient young man from Cincinnati, who was training for the Anglican priesthood. Goldhara grumped that the God in whom she did not believe had a lousy sense of humour, surrounding her on the Camino with *Christians*, of all things. Hume and I utterly failed to sympathize.

Over the next days I would spend hours in conversation with Hume, a hulking youngster whose buoyant personality made him agreeable company. I have met many trainee priests, but I had not previously encountered one for whom the structure, the fabric, of the priesthood so engaged his imagination. He seemed fascinated by the pageantry of the faith, and when he discovered that I had met several Archbishops of Canterbury in the course of my work he was thrilled. When I learned in turn that he had downloaded the whole of the Anglican Service Book onto his smartphone, I was left gaping. I am an Anglican by upbringing and training, but I have no profound affection for its liturgy and cycles, any more than its buildings and hierarchies: what matters to me are the people the Anglican Church attracts, for many of whom I have a great deal of respect.

This is true enough, but not the whole.

I have spent most of my life in the evangelical tradition, which elevates Scripture. Beyond that I have appreciated the insights and energies of the charismatic movement, with its emphasis on the presence and gifts of the Spirit. I have given such space as my abilities afford me to the insights granted by reason. Scripture, insight, reason: three legs of Wesley's famous quadrilateral,[66] of which the fourth is tradition, and of this I have been lamentably ignorant.

It is only in the last few years that I have started, not in the least to understand, but rather to resonate with, the richness of the tradition of Christian spirituality, drawing as it does on still deeper roots. At All Nations I had met Messianic Jews[67] for the first time, some of whom I now prize as friends. I loved the idea that they own an extra 2,000 years of wisdom and wrestling. But I have been careless of the wider resources available to me.

More recently, with Pen as my tutor, and having joined a fellowship with a much stronger liturgical tradition, I have started to discover the pulse behind the ecclesiastical year: the logic of Martinmas, Candlemas, and the Feast of St John: and so very much more.

What bothers me is not that I have disregarded such heartbeats, or that as a benighted urbanite I have not paid due attention to the agricultural calendar that in ancient days informed the structuring of the liturgical year. It is that I have been too horribly busy to listen. It is something of a

---

66 John Wesley, the evangelist and founder of the Methodist Church, gave pride of place to the Bible, describing himself as "a man of one book". However, doctrine, no matter how carefully drawn from Scripture, still has to accord with Christian tradition: we cannot be completely independent of our past. Faith – the step of becoming, then remaining, a Christian – is much more than assent to a set of ideas: it is a lived experience, a yielding to the Almighty. Bible, experience, and tradition must be capable of being defended rationally: hence the Wesleyan quadrilateral, a term coined in the twentieth century by Albert Outler.

67 Messianic Jews worship Jesus as Messiah and Lord while still retaining much of Jewish culture and liturgy. Four thousand years of history is an excellent excuse for a party. If you ever get invited to worship with them, don't pass up the opportunity.

characteristic, I fear, of the evangelical world: too busy doing the Lord's work to spend time with the deity in question. Too busy broadcasting to set the dial to *Receive*.

I have filled every waking minute with sixty seconds' worth of distance run,[68] as Kipling recommended. Often I have crammed in a few seconds more. I have worked early and late. Blessed with abundant energy, I spin plates for a living. If I do not receive a hundred emails a day I feel I am slacking.

This has not been something imposed upon me: I have chosen it. It's a common error. Rob Parsons, founder of Care for the Family, is fond of quoting, "Which of you, at the end of your life, will wish you had spent more time in the office?" It's a devastating question for the ambitious. My old mentor Edward England wrote at least twenty books, and one of the last was entitled *The Addiction of a Busy Life*. I have seen film (courtesy of *Top Gear*) of a remarkable Icelandic vehicle, essentially a high-geared truck with ridged wheels that rotate at such speed that, despite its weight, the truck can surge across the icy waters. I have been that truck, and it took a pilgrimage to drive the point home.

This has been my fear: that when you stop, you sink.

I have eschewed peace and contemplation. "Everything louder than everything else," sang Meatloaf, and how right he was. Screwtape esteemed Noise:

Music and silence – how I detest them both! How thankful we should be that ever since our Father

---

68 From the closing lines of Kipling's *If*:
"If you can fill the unforgiving minute
  With sixty seconds' worth of distance run,
Yours is the Earth and everything that's in it,
  And – which is more – you'll be a Man, my son."

> entered Hell – though longer ago than humans,
> reckoning in light years, could express – no square
> inch of infernal space and no moment of infernal
> time has been surrendered to either of those
> abominable forces, but all has been occupied by
> Noise – Noise, the grand dynamism, the audible
> expression of all that is exultant, ruthless, and virile.[69]

Noise stops you having to think, to consider your place in the Vortex. Whether it comes through your headset or your diary or your email provider, Noise is a drug, and an enemy. It cannot co-exist with the long, slow drumbeat of death and rebirth that lies at the heart of the sacred year.

And this too the silent Meseta revealed to me.

Hume was a genial soul, and now he and I turned our attention to twisting Goldhara's tail, very gently, as she muttered about archaic belief systems and those who exploit the credulous. Mack and Jim talked baseball: this was not their world. Meanwhile Jan, demonstrating practical sainthood, set about preparing a vast aromatic dish of pasta, and doled out the slicing of sausage and the grating of cheese to her idly chattering companions. Having had four children, she clearly considered herself the parent in this transaction, and we were pleased to play along: it was a magnificent feast, consumed overlooking the ancient tiles of the ancient town, draining from red to grey as the sun yielded to darkness.

---

69 *The Screwtape Letters*, C. S. Lewis, London: Geoffrey Bles, 1942.
Now published by HarperCollins. I discovered Screwtape while spending a year teaching at a French school, and filled a folder with notes. In all my many attempts to bring my library under stricter control, my collection of C. S. Lewis first editions has endured. More than any other writer, I owe that man an unpayable debt.

Castrojeriz – Frómista – Carrión de los Condes

Days 16 and 17

Over the next couple of days the landscape started to change. Fewer of the adjectival sunflowers; wheat makes an appearance as the soils improve.

I was on the road early again, trudging upwards – a sharp climb of over 100 metres in very short order – to the peak of the Alto Mostelares, and a return to the Meseta. The day's route would cross two canals: the Canal Pisuerga and then the Canal de Castilla.

I was excited to see this on the map, because canals are magic. They often provide great fishing, of course, but anyone who has ever spent a few hours on a narrowboat will attest to the subtle allure of banks, reeds, and bridges passing at four miles an hour. In Britain, canals reveal a secret world of eighteenth-century brickwork, old iron, forgotten wharfs, and ancient warehouses. And that is the bit above the surface. If you hang over the prow of a narrowboat, forty or fifty feet from the engine at the stern, you are gliding nearly silently into a tranquil watery world. It is easy to discern shoals of roach darting aside as the steel hull cuts the water, or spot a pike lurking beneath a lily pad – or, these days, American signal crayfish picking their way across the canal floor. (These rascals, introduced in the 1970s as a farmed species, have largely displaced the native British crayfish; DEFRA – the Department for Environment, Food and Rural Affairs – provides advice on how to trap them for the table. They are good eating, though DEFRA doesn't supply recipes.)

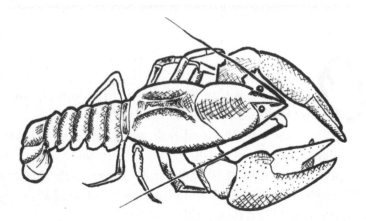

The British canal network is home to thousands of boat owners. If you do not have a permanent mooring (which can get expensive) you may stay fourteen days in any available spot before being required to move along. Many have discovered a luxury narrowboat is cheaper and more interesting than a small, drab house. Am I tempted? You bet.

Canals were once the equivalent of today's motorways,

an essential part of Britain's industrial revolution. In Spain canals never caught on to the same degree, but one of the few worthy of note is the eighteenth-century Canal de Castilla, along which the track ran for several kilometres on the approaches to Frómista. Outside Frómista stands a long flight of disused locks, and there are plans afoot to restore them and open the canal for boats right through its 127-mile length. Originally intended for the transport of wheat, the Canal de Castilla now has a noticeable current (not generally a feature of canals) and is used largely for irrigation. (The unremarkable Canal Pisuerga, built in 1932, is used exclusively for this purpose and has all the charm of a concrete pipe.)

I walked a goodly part of that day in company with Jack, a Canadian structural engineer turned church consultant. Jack had sold to his staff the successful company he built up, and now uses his planning skills assisting churches to configure their future – to dream dreams, and then put them into action. Over the following few days (he would be flying home partway through the Camino for his wife's sixtieth birthday) he and I spent hours in conversation. I listened in fascination to his stories of churches turned around, restored from slow decay to vibrant growth. A shrewd, quiet, independent spirit, he proved a fascinating companion. But then, to be fair, I didn't meet a dull pilgrim. No doubt they exist.

We ended the day at the Albergue Estrella del Camino in Frómista, a small town huddled around the enormous Iglesia de San Martin. This handsome Romanesque edifice, a national monument, attracts coachloads of tourists, its overwhelming stature a sharp contrast to the declining population. It is a decommissioned church, and it occurred to me to wonder where the locals turn for spiritual sustenance: vocations to the Catholic priesthood in Spain and France have fallen sharply in the last few decades, and parishes can contain several dozen churches serviced by one or two priests, with the consequence that a local mass is celebrated perhaps no more than three times a year. I wished I had posed the question to Jack: what can you do, when the entire edifice is so short of key personnel?[70]

That night the temperature fell sharply, and before the sun went down I resorted to the thick gilet Pen and my stepdaughters had bought me for the journey.

Goldhara and Theodore were both suffering from shin splints, and limping painfully. They reviewed their options, with neither willing to accept one obvious solution: to arrange, for seven euros, for your pack to be shipped ahead to the hostel of your choice. I think both felt it was cheating.

I had kept company for several kilometres that morning with Goldhara, before her legs grew too painful and she had to rest awhile. As we walked she told me a little more about her background. In the late 1980s she and her partner had determined to climb Mount Everest. She was watching him from base camp, through high-powered binoculars, when he lost his grip and fell to his death at 23,000 feet. "You

---

70   It ain't all bad everywhere. In England and Wales vocations to the Catholic priesthood have doubled since the turn of the millennium, though from a low base; a similar pattern has been reported from Ireland. The Church of England in 2012 reported a two-decade high in the number of young ordinands.

don't recover bodies from Everest," she added quietly as she concluded her brief dreadful tale. "We dropped him into a crevasse, so other climbers wouldn't have to look at him." She suffered from blackouts and bouts of vomiting for months afterwards.

That evening she was understandably downcast by so ghastly a memory, and I pondered what comfort I might offer my lovely atheist friend.

Christianity offers no reliable answer to the question of pain. There are various options, all of them not entirely satisfactory. You may speak of the Fall; you may say the Almighty's ways are hidden to mortals; you may opine about choices available in a universe where heights imply depths; you may muse on the nature of love and free will. As we found when my daughter Abbie's problems first began to manifest themselves, such reflections offer meagre consolation. I wanted to be able to howl, to hurl things at the Almighty:

My God, my God, why have you forsaken me?

So wrote David the king, in Psalm 22, providing the memorable words that Christ appropriated from the cross. One of the consolations of my faith is that it provides me with a target.

And, in sober earnest, I don't really need explanations when the tough times come: I need comfort. Most believers, I think, find an accommodation with the Infinite here. The cancer will return. The errant husband will not. Your son will not kick his drug habit. Your father will remain a monster. In the face of such austere truths, what matters to me is that, although the universe may be indifferent, its Creator is anything but; Jesus does not provide reasons, but He gets it, He is there. God become human; God, suffering too. There are no lullabies, no excuses, no proofs, but sometimes I can sense Him weeping with me, or – equally valuably – sharing a joke. It is, sometimes, enough.[71]

I could not offer such consolation to Goldhara. But then a memory surfaced. The previous day I had read in Tim Moore's *Spanish Steps*[72] about his joyful discovery of grappa, a robust and inexpensive Spanish brandy, and that night I proposed we should undertake a little research of our own. Jim (who had been regaling us with stories of fly-fishing for tarpon, a formidable game fish growing to sizes that make salmon seem minnows) thought this an altogether splendid development, and grappa accompanied our evenings thereafter.

Drink is not the answer, but it helps you evade the question, especially if taken in good company.

I mentioned wheat. The town name, Frómista, is derived from the Latin for cereal, *frumentum*, and this entire region was once the breadbasket of the Roman empire. The following day saw the start of a long section of Roman road.

I found this surprisingly upsetting. Roman traces abound in Britain, of course, but here their footprints seemed closer to the surface. I was reminded of a visit to Israel some

---

71   For a fuller exploration of this viewpoint, I recommend Francis Spufford's excellent *Unapologetic*, London: Faber & Faber, 2012. See especially chapter 5.

72   I had hundreds of books on my Kindle, but on the Camino read just the two: *Spanish Steps*, and Pen's *The Wilderness Within You*. Normally I am a book hound, consuming several each week, a habit since childhood. Now the waking hours were too full; books lost their appeal.

years previously when I had climbed to the rocky plateau of Masada, the location of the final stand of the Sicarii, a group of Jewish rebels. Josephus records that, after watching the Romans gradually construct a siege ramp up the cliffs, 960 rebels chose to end their lives there, each father slaying his wife and children.

It is still possible to lean over the walls and see clearly the squares of the temporary Roman encampment below, hacked by the legions out of the thin stony ground and preserved for two millennia in the desert air.

On the same trip I had walked the streets and pavements of Jerusalem that Christ had trod, and seen the vast stones, at which his disciples marvelled, still strewn across the ancient road where Roman soldiers had prised the Second Temple apart. The Temple had been fired in AD 70 during the sack of Jerusalem under Titus, and the troops had torn down the stones, seeking melted gold from the hangings which had seeped into the crevices. (The Arch of Titus, celebrating the campaign, still stands in Rome.)

Now, scant inches below the surface, lay the stones of the Roman roadway, set in place by locals drafted in by this same military power. The empire was sustained, not just by Spanish bread, but by Iberian silver and gold, and bullion from northern Spain would have been carried on this road. It must have been a vast operation, for much of the region is marshy, and stone would have had to be carted in over considerable distances. One long section had required 100,000 tons of rock, all trundled in from distant hills, to raise it above the winter floods. A gargantuan task; it did not require much imagination to appreciate that I was, entirely literally, walking over dead men's bones.

The local authorities had covered the Roman original for tedious tens of kilometres with roughly graded gravel, comprised of rocks just large enough to turn the ankle, requiring you to stare at your uninteresting feet for hour upon hour.

So passed another drab day, whose only real merit was that it came to an end. On such straight roads you can see just how far you have still to go. My respect grew sharply for those ancient soldiers, schlepping their packs and weapons along that unvarying length, devoid of shade, water, birdsong. This was in truth the most arduous portion of the Camino.

To make matters worse the nightmares had returned – the previous night at the Albergue Estrella del Camino had proved tough. Again Jane featured largely, and unfairly: it felt as if the drains of my soul were being opened afresh, with my ex-wife the nominated operative. The constant theme, again, was my failure to do something important. Morning came as a relief.

Mercifully, Hume's irrepressible humour enlivened the day, and I was grateful for his company. We quickly fell into conversation about his vocation to the priesthood, and with little to stay the eye we focused instead on what he had learnt over the previous year or so of parish experience about preaching, church politics, and the future of the faith.

Nevertheless, the dreams still haunted me whenever the conversation faltered, so I was pleased to reach the outskirts of Carrión de los Condes and the Albergue Santa Maria: an active religious community, right in the centre of the old, grey, stone-built town. The robed sisters stood ready at the entrance with glasses of tea and sweet pastries for arriving pilgrims: one of the warmest, most engaging welcomes of the entire Camino. We were invited to find bunks and stow our gear, then join the sisters for an informal meeting at 5.30. This turned out to be an unrehearsed singalong in several languages. Several dozen pilgrims crowded into the entrance hall and perched on the elegant wooden stairs. One young Italian girl, prevailed upon by her companions, had a voice of astounding sweetness; a moment of utter silence ensued when she finished, before the shouts and cheering began.

The sisters informed us that supper would be at 7.30, and encouraged us to bring food to share. I quickly lost my way in the winding alleys around the *albergue* before finding a grocery still open in mid-siesta to sell me sausage and bread. Like so many of the towns on the Camino, Carrión de los Condes has a glorious if bloody past[73] and a somewhat subfusc present, home to perhaps 2,500 souls where once 10,000 lived. But at least it is still alive. There is all the difference in the world between a monument – a fossil, maintained only for tourists – and a still-functioning community, which exists without your approval or attention. Sometimes the Camino felt like a walk through a museum. But here the steady transmutation of present into past was still happening.

Returning to the hostel I spent an agreeable hour or two with Robert – a French-Canadian scholar, for some years a prison chaplain. A generous-spirited, quirky individual, swift of wit and readily enthusiastic, he spoke equally fluently nasal French and oddly cadenced English, and was kind enough to lend me his iPad so I could book a flight home.

---

73 The counts of Carrión, for example, met an abrupt end at the hands of El Cid, after they had mistreated the latter's daughters.

I had held off from doing so until I felt reasonably sure of when I might actually reach Santiago, and the matter had been quietly gnawing away at me: by that point in the year flights are infrequent, and consequently full.

When I texted Pen with the date and time she was dismayed, a reaction I had not anticipated. To her it felt as if I were rushing my sabbatical. At the time it seemed simple pragmatism, because I didn't want to cool my heels in Santiago for days on end.

Looking back, she had a point. She has taught me a lot about staying in the moment – not reaching for the remote as soon as the credits roll; awaking slowly; chilling out, allowing a conversation to find its pace, rather than casting about for the next task. Goldhara (who followed the same itinerary as myself) would observe later, a little bleakly, that she felt she had rushed her journey. For my next pilgrimage I will allow more time to stop, and sip, and sniff.

Terradillos de los Templarios – Calzadilla de los Hermanillos

Days 18 and 19

The following morning promised little and fulfilled my expectations. The day's allocation was a longish stretch – 17 miles – from Carrión to Terradillos, much of it on the Calzada Romana, the Roman road. It was another featureless, monotonous day.

The only thing I found worth recording in the whole of that long hot tramp was a meeting with Mack, whom I found at one of the roadside picnic tables. We fell into conversation, and Mack, in a rare expansive mood, told me something of his past. He used to be a licensed hunter for the US Marines, chasing down and capturing guys who had absconded from the military and gone to the bad. However, his methods were too direct for Jimmy Carter's America, as Mack put it, and when his term ended his sergeant advised him not to re-enlist. He had then spent fifteen years on the road, hitching across the States, Jack Reacher reborn, never settling, never marrying, until a chance encounter led him to Hawaii and (to his surprise) a lucrative career in the property business. "I've had plenty of girlfriends," he told me, looking slightly puzzled. "I've stayed on good terms with most of 'em. They invite me to their weddings."

Mack didn't say much as a rule. He didn't need to.

The setting sun found me sitting in the garden of the Albergue Peregrinos Jacques de Molay, enjoying the last rays and massaging my tired feet.

I had chosen the *albergue* for its description in Brierley's guide: "The resident family follow in the traditions of the Templars by offering wholesome home cooking." This sounded good, and so it proved – a tasty and welcome meal washed down with a fiery green spirit poured from an unnamed bottle.

But I was also intrigued by the hostel's designation, honouring Jacques de Molay. The last Grand Master of the Knights Templar, he was burned at the stake aged seventy-two in Paris, at his request facing Notre Dame Cathedral, in March 1314. De Molay was the victim of the cowardice of Pope Clement V and the greed and ambition of the French king, Philip IV, who was deeply in debt to the Templars.[74] (Their refusal to grant him further loans probably precipitated the crisis.) Clement, who had been placed on the rocky papal throne by King Philip, obediently issued an instruction to the monarchs of Christian Europe to arrest all Templars on charges of heresy and hand them over to the Inquisition. In Britain King Edward II, who had met and liked Jacques de Molay, had little choice but to comply, but gave the British Templars two weeks' warning (and rounded up a scant few, whom he housed comfortably). De Molay's courageous death marked the end of the Templars, who for two centuries had waged bloody war to hold and protect the holy sites of Christian Jerusalem, at the urging of the faithful of Europe.[75]

---

74 The Knights Templar were a military and religious order, endorsed by the Roman Catholic Church around 1129. They were first set up to protect pilgrims to the Holy Land, and once they had received the backing of Bernard of Clairvaux at the Council of Troyes, rapidly became a favoured charity. Exempt from local laws and taxes, they reported only to the Pope, and would become leading troops in the Crusades. Their non-combatant members would handle the financial aspects – a nobleman going to the Crusades would often place his affairs in their hands – and as the Order grew secure and more wealthy it started providing letters of credit for pilgrims (it is likely that the Knights Templar were the first to use cheques). In the course of the next two centuries they established financial networks across Christendom. Their pre-eminence made them an attractive target for the French king.

75 See *The Telegraph* online: "A Stain on History", Dr Dominic Selwood, 18 March 2014.

This sickening story contains much to horrify, and is part of a centuries-long narrative providing ready ammunition to those who wish to pillory the Christian faith, and indeed all faiths. Burnings for heresy and witchcraft; persecution in turn of Catholics and Protestants, Quakers and Albigensians: anyone with a smattering of history can fill in the blanks. Thugs in power dressing their ambitions and hungers in the gaudy rags of religion; thugs whose grip on power is insecure, dragging my poor Saviour into position as a pretext for brutal repression; the Inquisition urging unbelievers into the light, as Spufford so memorably puts it, one fingernail at a time.

No religion is innocent of this behaviour. The service of the People is equally repressive: you question the Ongoing March of Progress? We have a bullet just for you. The disease of dogmatism knows no boundaries.

I refer you to my earlier comments on Gaia.

But there is something altogether more invidious at work here, beyond the mere exercise of power.

The history of organized religion deals in orthodoxy of creed and practice. Immense amounts of time and energy have been expended on establishing these boundaries, and the results have not been uniformly positive, because one man's conviction is another man's error. Terry Pratchett, one of my favourite authors, but no friend to my faith, describes the outcome of the internecine pizza wars of the Discworld. You can hear the scorn dripping from his chin:

> After the Schism of the Turnwise Ones and the
> deaths of some 25,000 people in the ensuing jihad
> the faithful were allowed to add one small bayleaf to
> the recipe.[76]

A goodly part of my life has been caught up in processes of creed, religious structures, and patterns of exclusion. Can women be priests? Should you speak in tongues? Can gays be Christians? Do Muslims automatically go to hell? Such willingness to pass judgment on others can easily become a uniting factor in communities and organizations alike – more than one major American evangelical group solicits funds to fight the supposed gay menace.[77]

I don't have answers, much of the time: I can formulate the arguments, but I am not truly persuaded that they matter, and I am quite certain that my opinion doesn't. I am a sinner, saved by the grace of Christ, and it is my privilege to share this joy, but I have no wish to light a bonfire under anyone.

Kipling has some crisp lines on dogmatism:

> Then I stripped them, scalp from skull, and my hunting-
> dogs fed full,
> And their teeth I threaded neatly on a thong;
> And I wiped my mouth and said, "It is well that they are
> dead,
> For I know my work is right and theirs was wrong."

---

76 Terry Pratchett, *Mort*, Corgi, 1987.

77 This is not a prescription for stability: how constructive is it to define yourself by what you are against? The British Prime Minister John Major once called for the creation of an anti-yob culture. That just means the yobs set the agenda.

> But my Totem saw the shame; from his ridgepole-shrine
>   he came,
> And he told me in a vision of the night: —
> "There are nine and sixty ways of constructing tribal lays,
> "And every single one of them is right!"[78]

Sadly, the Christian book world is as vulnerable as any other aspect of religion to the drawing of lines. Once, as a young editor and sales rep, I visited a London bookshop, and sold them a new youth resource from The Salvation Army. A month later I was asked to remove all the stock, because in one of the footnotes the author had quoted William Barclay, who was regarded as unsound. The Salvation Army exposed as dodgy: you read it here.

George Fox, founder of the Society of Friends, provides an insight which today lies at the core of the Quaker outlook on life:

> Be patterns, be examples in all countries, places,
> islands, nations wherever you come; that your
> carriage and life may preach among all sorts of
> people, and to them; then you will come to walk
> cheerfully over the world, answering that of God in
> everyone; whereby in them you may be a blessing,
> and make the witness of God in them to bless you.[79]

There is to my mind a truth here, that all of us have a hunger for the divine, and the capacity to respond.

However, the expression "that of God in everyone", which smacks slightly of the warm fuzzies, will sit uneasily with many Christians, much as many have objected to the "anonymous

---

78 "In the Neolithic Age", Rudyard Kipling
79 George Fox, 1656, www.quaker.org.uk/advices/fox

Christian" proposed by Jesuit theologian Karl Rahner, who put forward the inclusivist view that people who have never heard the Christian gospel might be saved through Christ. Evangelicals would point to Christ's unequivocal assertion, "I am the way and the truth and the life. No one comes to the Father except through me."[80] Both Fox and Rahner are also vulnerable to the charge of arrogance – imagine how an atheist might respond to being told that "there was a bit of God in her", or how a devout Sikh would react to being called an anonymous Christian, just as I would not take kindly to being described as a "hidden Muslim". Rahner has been criticized by evangelicals, Catholics, and liberals alike, but at least no one has tried to burn him.

All my life I have endeavoured, erratically and often unsuccessfully, to put myself under the authority of the Bible, and seek by prayer and study to understand Scripture. This I believe: if undertaken with humility, your studies into biblical truth, and your sincere devotions, will make you a more sympathetic, loving, and potent human being. Men and women of conviction are often impressive agents of social transformation, and it has been my good fortune to meet a number from whom the light of Christ shines. True godliness is attractive.

But if you use the Bible as a rigid rule book in every context, clinging to an over-literal understanding – or dress yourself in the trappings of faith while ignoring its heart – then that same study and prayer can lead to dogmatism, and at the end of that road lies a smouldering match.

My beloved Pen Wilcock, who has lived through more

---

80 John 14:6, NIV

traumas than many, expresses it thus: my karma ran over my dogma.

Terradillos de los Templarios was formerly a stronghold of the Templars, but nothing remains of their long presence, other than their name. The simple village is now notable for the single fact that it lies precisely halfway between St Jean Pied-de-Port, and Santiago de Compostela.

I slept well that night, woke early, and full of bounce set off into the dawn, only to realize ten minutes later that I had left my headgear hanging on the *albergue*'s wall. With a sigh I retraced my steps to seek an old friend. My battered canvas bush hat, purchased years previously in the American Rockies, was proving wonderfully durable, the broad brim sheltering its fragile owner from the Meseta's sun and Galicia's downpours.

A few kilometres outside Terradillos the Camino crosses yet another boundary, into the province of León, or Llión if speaking the official language of Leonese. Ahead lay the city of that name. That night I told my daughter Abbie about this. "You've got it wrong, Dad," she texted back. "Leon lives in Birmingham." She was quite right: her ex-boyfriend Leon had moved north.

That day, and for much of the rest of my journey, I fell into further agreeable French company. An hour or so into the morning I caught up with a couple in their fifties, he with ponytail and piratical scarlet headscarf, she with a mop of curls. Scallop shells dangled from their packs, inscribed with a start date in mid-August. On enquiry I discovered that Pierre and Brigitte had set off from Le Puy a couple of months previously. "By the time we reached Spain we had a thousand kilometres in our legs," commented Brigitte. She was a nurse, he a retired schoolteacher. They were easy companions on the Way, comfortable in their skins, and I spent hours yarning with them.

The road was still proving tiresome, however, and it grew more so as we approached the outskirts of Sahagún, site of a famous Benedictine monastery of the tenth century which ministered to pilgrims, and indeed another community effectively called into being by the Camino. Sahagún's drab outskirts, dedicated to light industry, were as wearing to the feet as to the spirit, but I was transfixed by a graveyard of vast, extinct agricultural machinery close to the town centre. There lay huge listing hulks of rust-streaked blue, red, and yellow metal, tractors and harvesters and trucks, sagging tyres and broken windscreens, pools of oil and swaying grass, all corralled tightly into a lot like sad broken-down old nags and surrounded by chain-link fence so they couldn't escape.

The *albergue* in Calzadilla was a basic but cheerful affair, and the hosts welcomed us warmly. Brigitte made the poor *anglais* a cup of tea, the first in weeks. The hostel had a large drawing of a bed bug just inside the main door, informing the blighters that they were banned from this establishment. Brigitte admitted she had been attacked the previous night, so she and Pierre were asked to sleep in an adjacent room.

The evenings were getting chilly; the crowded reception area was heated by a roaring wood stove, delighting the gathered pilgrims. In pleasing synchronicity, that night I read chapter 11 of Pen's *The Wilderness Within You*, a series of conversations with Jesus. In it she records Christ's advice on the lighting of fires:

"Fires," he observes, "are all about bridges and spaces. If you want a fire to catch, you need both. Things have to be so set up that there's something in place as a bridge to carry the flame from one to the next, but leaving spaces so the fire can breathe and the flame is not suffocated."

I know him well enough by this time to grasp that he is, and is not, discussing wood, flame and newspaper. He means people. He means Holy Spirit. He means souls. This is the man who came to set the whole world ablaze. He knows how to start a fire.

Perhaps George Fox is right: there is something of God in everyone, waiting to be ignited.

Mansilla de las Mulas – León – Villavante

Days 20 and 21

The following day offered another gruelling trudge along the Calzada Romana. The roughly graded gravel required constant attention, which distracted the eye from the dead sunflowers. Not a butterfly, not a bird, not a lizard, not an ant. Again, the eye cast inwards; this time, and more constructively, I found sufficient peace and space for prayer. I walked and prayed, prayed and walked, offering my loved ones and my colleagues to the Almighty's care. Between whiles my imagination populated the drear terrain with the ghosts of marching soldiers – both Muslim and Christian forces used the road in the era of Charlemagne – and with the shades of the millions who succeeded them over the centuries. Wisps, insubstantial as the roadside grass, insubstantial as this chronicle. The feet have vanished, but the road remains.

Mansilla de las Mulas, that night's destination, has strong equine associations: *Mansilla* means "hand on the saddle", and the tag "*de las Mulas*" refers to the community's former fame as a livestock market. The old town is still contained within the medieval walls, and the narrow meandering streets proved a boon after the vastness of the prairie, their human scale keeping the Vortex at bay. Just outside the town I caught up with Jack and Robert, and stopped with them for a beer and *bocadillo*. I bade Robert farewell; he was planning to catch a taxi to León.

The *albergue* in Mansilla was exceptionally cheap, and exceptionally basic; I washed my clothes and spread them optimistically to dry in the hostel courtyard, setting them to catch the thin warmth of the October sun. Damp clothing was becoming a daily reality. Then I wandered down to the bridge over the Rio Esla, and watched trout rising to the evening's flies.

It had been a flat hike, not particularly demanding, but I felt transparent with fatigue. My left shoulder blade and my pack were still at war, and my knees were interjecting the occasional violent twinge. The landscape had offered no distraction, and the day had worn me thin.

In circumstances of such tedium meals become more than punctuation: they become oases. That night I found a restaurant with Goldhara and Jan, Mack, Jim, Hume, and two friends of Jim's – Mike and Terry – a cordial couple who had flown in from South Dakota to spend a few days with him on the road. "A convivial meal," I noted in my Moleskine. It would be quite proper to regard this chronicle as a record of meals devoured and shared. *Qu'il est gourmand, ce mec*.

The following morning I set out with Hume, and after breakfast in a small, drab bar – a regular but unremarkable feature of the Camino – we fell into company with a Dutch gent in his sixties. He seemed eager to talk, and the polite initial questions provoked an extraordinary story. With little prompting he explained that his daughter had two girls by different men. His daughter's husband, father of her second child, had abandoned her for another woman. The two youngsters were now being raised by our companion and his wife (he had walked from Holland, a distance requiring months, so just at that point his wife was shouldering the burden).

However, his errant son-in-law had a father, also Dutch, from whom the absent young man was entirely estranged, and the father was now living in Spain, with a Spanish woman.

Our new friend described how a few days previously he had tracked this gentleman down to a house outside Burgos. He had turned up at this man's door, quite unannounced, and informed him that they had a granddaughter in common. After some period of bogglement he was invited in. Many explanations and photos followed, with a phone call to Holland to confirm the story. A bond was forged, and the little girl had a new grandfather.

I looked at our thin, bearded, wholly ordinary companion with admiration for his compassion and tenacity. He was still glowing with satisfaction, as indeed he should.

Ahead lay León, the third big city of the Camino after Pamplona and Burgos. León is a corruption of "Legion" – the Romans got there first and made it the base for their VIIth Legion. The city, like many in Spain, has been conquered and reconquered by Visigoths, Moors, and Christians, each leaving their architecture and their genes. León enjoys fiestas all year long, including the ubiquitous running bulls, but we managed to miss them, slipping quietly that night into the Albergue Santa Maria de Carbajal, a considerable hostel of 132 beds run by a Benedictine order. As we entered León we hooked up with Jack, our Canadian engineer, for a last evening together. The following morning he would be catching the early bus to Madrid, and flying back for his wife's birthday.

I loved León, a major city but altogether more human in scale than Burgos, filled with medieval buildings and bustling with little boutiques: it reminded me of York. Jack, Hume, and I found a football bar for the evening. The match on screen (between two European teams) was not one that any of us cared about, and conversation lagged, with Jack's impending departure heavy upon us.

Though the Benedictine order that runs the hostel is enclosed, the sisters had invited us to share their worship and participate in that night's service. So we headed back to Compline at 9.30, joining a surprisingly large group of pilgrims, to be shepherded down the street to the church a few hundred yards away. A fluently multilingual nun handed out booklets in the appropriate tongue and drilled us in the responses.

While the crowd of pilgrims waited to enter the sanctuary, a young French/American couple were seated to one side, kissing passionately: I would meet them again at journey's end, still entwined. The Camino is a genial meeting ground for those open to love.

Compline is the final office of the day: it signifies the end of the working day and is a quiet, meditative service offering a chance to reknit mind, spirit, and body. In monasteries it ushers in the Great Silence of the night. It includes psalms, often sung; responses and scriptural readings. The settings were unfamiliar to me but the words were not, since I had been helpfully handed an English text, and I emerged refreshed despite the melancholy evening.

As we left the church we filed past a well-executed, life-size supine sculpture of Christ after He had been taken down from the cross. Before us lay every laceration, every puncture, every thorn. No excruciating detail had been omitted. My eyes slid away, and I found myself ashamed at my revulsion.

Yet I felt awkward at this emphasis on the dead, rather than the resurrected, Christ. This aspect of Spanish Catholicism was apparent in every church I visited: a glorification, almost a relishing, of the suffering Saviour, and the suffering martyrs. One French woman I met confessed that she too, a Catholic from infancy, found it oppressive. Yet the nuns and priests I met seemed good, holy, competent people, focused and prayer-filled, not obviously overshadowed by the darker aspects of their faith. Perhaps such statuary allowed them to externalize the more dreadful aspects of the Christian story.

Of course, such art allows the onlooker to stay with the horror of the moment, not surround it with words like resurrection or grace.

On our way back to the dormitory I ran into Jacques, my one-armed friend from a couple of weeks before, and greeted him with real pleasure: I had missed his witticisms and sweet temper. It was, however, a case of hail and farewell, as he was staying in León for a few days to savour the history and the Gaudi architecture. I was tempted to join him, but the road called. I will return.

Jan and Jim, Mack and Goldhara, Terry and Mike had all booked rooms at the Parador in León, the luxury hotel featured in *The Way*. I was tempted for a few moments, but I was deep in pilgrim mode and decided to stick with Benedictine austerity. Fantastic breakfast, they informed us later, but the Parador – accustomed as it must be to pilgrims – was evidently slightly ill at ease with its regular clientele of shabby backpackers: it's a posh joint, and shepherded our road-worn friends away from the handsome reception area.

Knowing none of this, Hume and I nabbed a couple of bottom bunks and opined with effortless superiority that we were entirely comfortable with our crowded dormitory.

Early the following morning we made our way out through the dozing city towards La Virgen del Camino, a suburb on the western outskirts, where at the obligatory drab café we paid a ransom in euros for juice and croissants. The route led straight past the Parador, and we made uncouth comments about our companions lolling in swinish luxury. The first kilometres took us through industrial outskirts, factories and warehouses, vacant lots, yet more chain-link fence. Then, after examining the map, we resolved to eschew the official route, which closely followed the tedious busy highway, and struck out across country for the hamlet of Villar de Mazarife.

Hume, a chunky young wolf, moved briskly, and we reached Villar before one o'clock, where we tracked down beer and sandwiches before deciding to head on. At Villavante, a further 10 kilometres off, we found beds for the night at the Albergue Santa Lucia. Here we lucked out: a nicely designed modern hostel run by a nicely designed young woman, with an arrogant parrot called Coco. It had been an unremarkable day, and notably damp in its latter stages, but we had covered 32 kilometres.

The unremitting fields of maize came a close second to dead sunflowers for extreme dullness, and the day was chiefly notable for a searching conversation with Hume about speaking in tongues. I told him what I understood of the practice, and about my own limited experience. I had received the gift of tongues decades previously at a pre-Lambeth Conference organized by the charismatic Fountain

Trust,[81] and it remains a precious part of my spiritual life. I am somewhat reluctant to use it in public worship, because it feels too private, but mowing the lawn is a great opportunity to sing in tongues.

I relish charismatic worship. The other memory of that conference is of dancing in the central aisle of Canterbury Cathedral, arm in arm with a portly African archbishop in handsome crimson robes, who despite his diminutive size – he was at least a foot shorter – then seized me by the waist, shouting in joy and praise, and swung me around and around.

Despite this history I chickened out of offering to pray for Hume to receive this gift, a hesitation I afterwards regretted.

Why so shy? I am not normally backward in meeting and greeting, and frequently too willing to leap into a conversation. But something held me back, perhaps a sense that this was holy ground, perhaps an awareness that I am no infallible guide to the spiritual world. Peter Lawrence, an Anglican minister for whom I published several books in the late 1980s, once observed that the central thing in prayer ministry is to pray: if nothing happens, you may look like a twerp, but who cares? If the Spirit intervenes, then to God be the glory, and that's the important bit.

Clare de Graaf, in *The 10-Second Rule*,[82] argues that you

---

81 The ecumenical Fountain Trust was started in 1964 to promote the charismatic renewal by Michael Harper, a young Church of England priest. It was exceptionally influential and presented a number of well-supported conferences. In 1980 the Trust decided to dissolve itself, considering that its primary task was complete. Its magazine, *Renewal*, was subsequently acquired by Edward England, who in due course passed it to me; in 2000 I sold it to *Christianity* magazine.

82 *The 10-Second Rule*, Clare de Graaf, Oxford: Monarch Books, 2013.

should just do the next thing that you are reasonably certain Jesus wants you to do. If you think longer than ten seconds, you will find an excuse not to do it. It's a simple, memorable way to remain obedient to the voice of the Spirit. I should have remembered it that day.

Sorry, Hume. I pray you find your own path to this gift.

That night we ate with John, an elderly Irish builder from Balham in South London. He was full of proud stories about his children, delivered in a broad brogue that left Hume boggling. His daughter was a businesswoman and a linguist; his son, at thirty-seven, the headmaster of a tough London school. A younger daughter, also a gifted linguist, had died, he told us, adding, "She's why I walk." Despite crocked knees and a weak heart, he had undertaken one pilgrimage after another, searching for an elusive peace. He had no time at all for the church: the road was his sanctuary.

Astorga – Rabanal del Camino

Days 22 and 23

*H*ume and I had stolen a few kilometres from that day's journey by our efforts the previous afternoon, which proved just as well, because with the dawn the rain set in, the first truly pounding downpour of my Camino. My absurd poncho proved just as useless as before, transforming itself into such a sweat bath that perspiration was dripping from my cuffs while we were yet hours away from our destination. What a pair of drowned rats.

We stopped for a breakfast croissant in Hospital de Órbigo. The expanse of the Rio Órbigo is traversed at this point by a long, loping medieval bridge set on a steady succession of arches. Built in the thirteenth century to replace a Roman original, it is, says Brierley, one of the great historical landmarks of the Camino.

In the Holy Year 1434[83] a famous tournament took place at the site. A knight from León, Don Suero de Quiñones, nicknamed Él del Passo (The Man of the Pass), with ten companions, challenged all comers – an inconvenience, given that the bridge would normally have been thronged with pilgrims. Knights from across Europe accepted the challenge, failing comprehensively, and in the course of the next month Don Suero accumulated 300 lances. There is a story that he had been crossed in love, and the feat of arms restored his sense of honour. One felt his reluctant lady had a point. Don Suero achieves a mention in *Don Quixote*, the satire on romantic chivalry.

Thereafter the Way proved uneventful, devoid of knights. The landscape was changing back to mixed arable crops intermingled with vineyards and orchards, more often than not untended. An image sticks in the mind: an apple tree, groaning with fruit, sitting behind a locked gate in a deserted courtyard, windfalls thickly littering the ground. Someone had planted that tree just a few decades previously.

Northern Spain, in one tree.

Astorga was wonderful, however; a substantial community tightly packed within its medieval walls, located on the junction of several routes – the Camino Frances and the Calzada Romana cross the Vía de La Plata, the

---

83 "In the Roman Catholic tradition, a Holy Year, or Jubilee, is a great religious event. It is a year of forgiveness of sins and also the punishment due to sin, it is a year of reconciliation between adversaries, of conversion and receiving the Sacrament of Reconciliation, and consequently of solidarity, hope, justice, commitment to serve God with joy and in peace with our brothers and sisters. A Jubilee year is above all the year of Christ, who brings life and grace to humanity." The first ordinary Jubilee was proclaimed in 1300 by Pope Boniface VII. www.vatican.va

ancient Roman Silver Route traversing western Spain from north to south. The town's former Roman overlords built generously, and close to the municipal hostel where we found beds for the night there is a considerable excavation of a Roman villa.

Astorga is the regional capital for the Maragato people, a cultural remnant with distinctive dress and cuisine. No one is entirely sure of their origin, and they are a group marooned by the surges of history. Their name may derive from captive Moors, "Mauri", forced to labour in the region's gold, silver, and tin mines; they may hail from the time of the Visigoths and their king Mauregato; perhaps they are descended from the Berber tribes who came to Spain during the Moorish invasion in the eighth century. There are only about 4,000 of them now, scattered in nearby villages and doing what they can to resist assimilation.

The town is a tourist destination, packed with exquisite boutiques and patisseries. Astorga is notable not only for its chocolate (a local speciality) and its cathedral, but for a spectacular confection of a building by Gaudi called the Bishop's Palace, which to my unappreciative gaze looked as if Disney had commissioned a wedding cake from Tim Burton: only the bats were missing.

I left my detested poncho, dried and neatly packed, with the hostel's Japanese warden, asking her to give it to some deserving traveller: an act of shameful hypocrisy, made worse by the decent lady's thanks. As soon as the shops opened after the siesta I bought myself a proper cagoule in bright blue.

After an exquisite late lunch of savoury chorizo braised in red wine – perhaps the most delicious single dish I ate in

Spain – I failed to meet my French and American friends that evening and dined alone, consuming a pizza notable for its cheese content. Astorga, in fact, was something of a gastronomic milestone, as the following morning I encountered hot chocolate accompanied by *churros*, a Spanish delicacy – a mix of flour, sugar, cinnamon, and oil piped out and baked: astonishingly palatable, but to be ingested with a health warning. Such specialities need their own context, as any imbiber of *retsina* will confirm: utterly appropriate when sampled next to a harbour in Mykonos; an affront to the palate in a London Greek eatery. Likewise *churros*, delicious on a cold Spanish October morning, but a sad disappointment the following year outside a café at Greenbelt.

That evening I was standing in the hostel kitchen, vainly rearranging my damp laundry, when my phone rang: a most welcome call from my wife. It was a delight to hear her voice, and she had news. Not only had her seventh novel, *The*

Breath of Peace,[84] been published through the good offices of her agent and our friend Chip MacGregor, but she and her mother had hatched a plan to combine resources and buy a magnificent property a little further inland, with space for all. (This ambition would come to naught, but the possibility kept my mind racing over the next few days.)

The following morning was Abbie's birthday. I texted a greeting and received one back, warning me to be careful in the mountains. Abbie's concern was justified: we had left the Meseta behind us, and stood on the borders of Galicia. Galicia was wet, everyone assured me, and with a sense of things to come I wormed my way into damp trousers, socks, shirt, and boots.

The depression engendered by this intimate soggy encounter was soon dispelled by Astorga's chocolate, and with the rising dawn I set off into the mist. Now the track started to climb, with mountain ranges on the horizon, and I once more found myself leaning into the ascent, each step a foot or more higher than the last, ridge after ridge, bounding across the erratic stony ground and relishing my capacity to leap up the rocky slopes after days of plod. In truth it was not an arduous journey, and shortly after midday I found myself standing in the middle of Rabanal del Camino, a small gem of a village dedicated to preparing pilgrims for the following day: the highest point on the Way.

The Confraternity of St James has a hostel in Rabanal. I was minded to stay there, but as I wandered up through the steep, narrow main street and greeted snoozing cats, I was hailed by the lovely Wine Sisters. So I booked myself into

---

84 Since released by Lion Fiction.

the hostel they had found (basically a private home with a welcome wood stove),[85] then joined them at a roadside café to enjoy a beer, a bowl of gazpacho, and the afternoon sun.

For a while I chatted to Angelo, a sparky young German with a fluent command of English. We fell to talking about the Cruz de Ferro, the Cross of Iron, which we would find at the summit of the following day's ascent. The tradition is that each traveller brings from home some item, usually a stone, to place at the foot of the Cross. My stepdaughter Hebe had taken the trouble to pick up a pebble from Hastings beach and paint upon it the *coquille Saint Jacques*, the scallop shell of the Camino: it was waiting safe in my pack. Angelo, an intriguing combination of amateur photographer and professional wrestler, had brought along a Papa Smurf, but had given him to a small child.

An hour later Mike and his wife Terry, Jim's friends, rolled in, looking really quite fresh for Camino novices. While Mike booked their beds, Terry confessed that she and he had taken a cab from Astorga, ducking in shame below the window as they passed Jim on the road. "Ah, the Carmino," responded Angelo.

Mike joined us, and as the collection of glasses accumulated through the afternoon he and Terry yarned about hunting, fishing, guns, and the best way to dress out a deer; about the extremes of climate in South Dakota, which in the space of months can oscillate from -58°F to 120°F. Part Sioux, Mike happily described how he had obtained a DVD of Kevin Costner's *Dances with Wolves*, which he watched with his mother, a Sioux speaker. At the point in

---

85 And a coffee machine with a piece of Spanglish to treasure: "Place the glass before pulsating." I did.

the film where Costner's character Lt John Dunbar joins the Indians, his mother had burst out laughing, gasping, "He speaks like a woman!" Apparently in the Sioux tongue the gender of the speaker determines the form of the language, and the Native American consultant on the film was female.

Later that evening Jim wanted to know what you had to say when you reached the Cruz de Ferro. I raised my eyebrows in query. "In the film they say a prayer," he amplified. "What do you say?"

He was right. In Sheen's *The Way* the characters climb to the foot of the Iron Cross and say their piece. There was no set form of words, I assured him, but he was clearly not entirely satisfied, and out of his comfort zone. So, before turning in that night, I composed him a prayer on a page torn from my Moleskine:

> Holy Spirit of God
>   With this stone I express my past, my present, and my future.
>   I acknowledge before you that things have not gone as planned. Sometimes I have been at fault.
>   Take all that I have been, and all that I can be, and make of me the jewel you had in mind.
>   Amen.

He was pleased. The following day he, Jan, and Goldhara sat opposite the Cruz an hour or so after I had passed by, and drank a bottle or two of wine together. "It was communion," said Goldhara.

Months later he sent me a scan of the scrap of paper, creased from his wallet.

By this stage Mack had left us. A man of immense energy, he could not reconcile himself to our modest pace, and in the course of a day he simply vanished ahead. Jim and he planned to meet in Portugal, or North Africa.

Molinaseca – Villafranca del Bierzo

Days 24 and 25

Our route the following morning would take us over the highest point on the Camino – at 4,940 feet considerably higher than the peak of Ben Nevis.[86]

The road out of Rabanal led upward, setting the tone for the days ahead. Heavy mist blanketed the mountains, cutting visibility to a few tens of metres and bedewing eyebrows and beard. It was cool, but not chilly, the dawn air pure.

First sparsely, then more lavishly, little congregations of purple cup-like flowers appeared: autumn crocus, springing leafless out of the harshest ground. The first sudden bursts of beauty in a stony featureless waste made me catch my breath: an unlooked-for blessing, precious and vulnerable.

The path winds up through forest to the little village of Foncebadón, largely abandoned, but now starting to stir back to life with the revival of the Camino. As the last

---

86 Ben Nevis, at 4,409 feet, is the highest mountain in the British Isles.

tumbledown house fell behind in the mist I saw a familiar pair of backs ahead, and paused with Pierre and Brigitte to exchange greetings: they each had their stone handy, ready to deposit. It felt entirely right to have their company for this moment.

Up again, around the brow of the hill, and there before us, looming out of the cloud at the summit of our journey, stood the Cruz de Ferro.

The place was a *mess*.

Thousands upon thousands have deposited their pebbles, their watches and scarves, plastic-wrapped photos and rusting lockets, pendants and decaying belts. Sagging soggy wisps of garish silk and nylon festooned the weathered pole that supports the iron cross. There were boots, greetings, figurines, tin mugs with plastic flowers, all stretching for tens of yards, a cairn of mementos. Angelo's Papa Smurf would have felt entirely at home.

It was unbelievably untidy, but it was also a shrine. Every single item had been carried there with love and laid down in benediction. I stood, stared, and wept, for the hope, the kindness, the longing, the regret, the thanksgiving and celebration that had powered so many pilgrims. It was a place of vulnerability, where princes and shop assistants might stand together, equal on this scruffy holy ground.

We set down our pebbles and rummaged for our cameras, to take our places in the stream of witness. Then we simply stood, silent.

Centuries later I realized I was getting cold. The wind, blowing the mist away, revealed the mountains around and the village ahead, and my shirt and trousers were soaked.

Waving adieu to my friends I set off across the mountaintop, down through dripping forests heavy with brilliantly crimson rowan berries, to the largely deserted twelfth-century hamlet of Manjarín, one of two communities on the Camino with an official population of one, a former pilgrim who, since 1993, has been renovating an abandoned house and offers – for a *donativo* – a hostel with very basic facilities and a signpost listing distances to a spectrum of improbable destinations: Chihuahua, Machu Picchu, Trondheim. Tomás Martinez, the *hospitalero*, describes himself as one of the last Templar knights, serving food and offering refuge to pilgrims through this high and lonely place: a modern hermit, poor in substance but rich in grace.

A few kilometres further, the track falls off a cliff, or nearly so. In the space of a few heartbeats you descend hundreds of metres across ankle-snapping rock, distracted at every step by the wonderfully vertiginous peaks as they emerge from the mist, shreds of cloud still clinging to the high forests.

Clamped to the hillside below lies the hamlet of Acebo, featuring a single principal street and several bars and *albergues*. As the altitude diminishes so the temperature increases, and now the sense of abandonment began to recede: almost every handsome stone house had been restored. The houses are quite distinctive, most featuring a first-floor balcony and a pair of stout doors, presumably for livestock, below. Right across Spain I had noticed the ancient doors, graced with formidable hinges and girded with heavy studs: they would not have looked out of place at a Black Sabbath fraternal. Now the ironwork shone brightly, the October sunlight glinting off the polished bolts and bars.

I stopped for a sandwich, then on the road out of the

village passed a skeletal sculpture of a bicycle, a memorial to one of the many pilgrims killed on the Camino. This was not bike-friendly terrain.

That night I made landfall in Molinaseca, and spent a while chatting in a bar to a Brit called Roger, a retired property consultant. I asked him to explain what had led him into this profession, and in the course of his explanation he mentioned, with stiff pride, that he had, since retirement, completed an HND (Higher National Diploma) in furniture design and manufacture. He was an austere, self-contained sort of cove, but I pressed him to tell me about his work and he unbent a trifle, describing a dressing table of intriguing complexity.

The conversation set me pondering. I have for years enjoyed banging pieces of wood together, and two or three of my shelves have actually stayed on the wall. I particularly like making passably useful furniture from recycled timber.

Back home I was facing a choice. I was nearing the point where my minuscule pension would kick in, and Pen was keen that I should stop my endless disruptive oscillation between Hastings and Oxford. I still loved my job – publishing is fun – but you can only truly publish for your own culture, and the time was approaching when I ought to make way for sharper, younger brains. When I started at Hodder, to be a publisher was still – just slightly – a game for gentlemen, a little light editing before lunch at the club; but these days it is hard work, fast and technical and competitive. By paddling furiously I could keep my thinning locks above water, but for how much longer?

So what might I do instead, while liver and lights still functioned? An HND in furniture design sounded just the ticket.

Molinaseca is another delightful gem, its narrow medieval streets full of character and cats. I had identified the Albergue Santa Marina as the designated dosshouse of the night, anticipating an evening of careful attention to its vaunted modern facilities. It stood some way out of town, and proved a soulless establishment of metal and stripped pine, designed for pilgrim processing. But it was clean and warm, and the beer was cold, even if the meal provided by the management proved devoid of personality or flavour.

That night the entire hostel, all four floors, was awakened, sometime around 1.00 a.m., by a loud thumping on the front door. All hostels have fairly strict curfew arrangements, lights out as a rule around 10.00 p.m., since weary footsloggers need their rest. One lady had drunk deeply of the local vintages, and, arriving on the doorstep hours after the doors were locked, she made her disapproval felt. The proprietor was absent, or unwilling to stretch a point. Bang bang, swear bang, abuse bang, scream bang, kick rattle bang, for the better part of an hour before the police arrived. It was the only instance of truly uncouth behaviour I encountered on the Camino.

The following morning I realized, as I entered Ponferrada, that I should have pushed on the additional five kilometres the previous night. Ponferrada is a considerable bustling town where the old medieval settlement occupies most of the high ground around the imposing castle. There were art exhibitions, historical artefacts, wonderful tall stone bridges, and as I wandered through it the next morning looking for a bank to restore my depleted money belt I found myself immersed in modern Spain, old and new, in a way that had escaped me since León. Ponferrada is the capital of El Bierzo, yet another semi-autonomous region, whose microclimate – mild, low altitude, with slightly acidic soils – has proved extraordinarily beneficial for wine production, which probably explained the woman of the previous night.

I do not have many regrets from my Camino, but not to have stopped and savoured the wines of El Bierzo is among the few. "To drink the wine in the land where the grape is grown", in Shirley Valentine's immortal phrase.

I spent much of the stretch to Villafranca in the company of Jan and Goldhara. We had long passed the stage of idle conversation; that day I learned that Goldhara has a son who is mentally ill, and from whom she has to conceal her whereabouts, such is his behaviour.

At one level these stories wrench the heart. Yet this is much less than the whole truth. Goldhara is now married to a rather brilliant boffin who is ensuring that America's wilderness areas can be traversed using GPS. She (and Jan) live life absolutely to the full, as I learned when Goldhara described a truly hairy raft trip through the Grand Canyon.

One of the joys of the Camino, I think, is to meet so many folk who have refused to sit down by the waters and weep – or, having wept, have climbed to their feet once more. I heard some distressing stories along the Way. But I didn't meet any victims.

Villafranca proved another delight, a small town full of history and imposing stone buildings. It came as no surprise to learn that medieval pilgrims unable to continue to Santiago were able to receive an equivalent absolution here. It must have been a tempting prospect, for tomorrow the road led upwards into Galicia. Note that word: upwards.

I found a bed for the night across the bridge over the Río Burbia at the wonderful Albergue de la Piedra, the Hostel of the Rocks: as full of character as the *albergue* in Molinaseca had been bland. The hostel wraps around the crags lining the river valley, spurs of rock intruding right into the lobby and the storeys above. I dumped my gear, showered and changed, then headed back over the bridge into town, for tonight we were to say farewell to Mike and Terry: they had responsibilities at home, and Mike's business needed him. I was sad to see them go, and it was close to curfew before I tore myself away from the convivial group, padding over the damp stone back to my bunk through darkness and rising mist.

"Wherever you stay," concludes Brierley on Villafranca, "make sure you get a good night's sleep to fortify yourself for the strenuous but stupendous hike the next day."

O'Cebreiro – Triacastela
Days 26 and 27

The morrow would prove, apart from the first day's appalling scramble over the pass to Roncesvalles, the steepest and toughest of the entire Camino, a long winding road up the Valcarce valley.

The destination was O'Cebreiro, the mountain village where Don Elías Sampedro had been the parish priest: he who had devised the system of yellow arrows upon which the modern Camino depends. His bespectacled bust presides over the church square. This was yet to come.

Galicia, as I have mentioned, is a place of enduring wetness. The prevailing winds, from the south and west, gather a heavy burden of moisture as they cross the Atlantic, and when they rise above the peaks of Galicia and the air turns colder, they relieve themselves of their bounty. Galicia receives twice the average rainfall of, say, Manchester. It's wonderfully verdant, the mountains cloaked in forest.

That night I noted in my Moleskine that the day had started wet, and got wetter. Even my indestructible bush hat gave way under the onslaught. For the first part of the astonishing climb I slogged along in just a T-shirt, appreciating the cool drizzle, but as the path rose up through the clouds and the precipitation increased I grew both soggier and colder, and ended by breaking out my Astorgan cagoule.

The scenery, when the rain clouds parted, was straight out of *The Lord of the Rings*, or, as it was formerly known, New Zealand: shrouded peaks plunging to deep green valleys, cataracts spewing down the mountainsides. Galicia is called "the land of a thousand streams".

Near Vega de Valcarce, a small village just before the road starts upward, the route leads beneath the imposing arches of the A6 motorway. Not for the first time the Camino offered a sense of two worlds passing, barely aware of the other's existence. I crossed a small hurrying river, glancing over the parapet to spot a trout holding station in the lee of a rock, and set my face to the mountain. A small house of local stone squatted beside the track, with a large sign offering horseback rides up to O'Cebreiro. Looking at the stomach-clenching slope ahead I was briefly tempted. An hour or so later I had to perch to one side of the path to avoid a string of relieved ponies ambling back down, their saddles and panniers empty, the enterprising chevalier bringing up the rear.

As the path climbed, my spirits – already cheerful – rose and rose. Despite the weather, slope, and heavy pack, my reconstituted body was proving equal to the challenge, and I started to sing:

All around my hat I will wear the green willow
And all around my hat for a twelve month and a day

> **And if anyone should ask me the reason why I'm**
> **wearing it**
> It's all for my true love who's far, far away.

I warbled loudly to the half-glimpsed mountains, giving thanks for Steeleye Span. I couldn't remember the rest of the verses, but who cared? Sometimes a song is the only response.

Galicia is a well-watered land in more than one sense; the regular village bars dotted along the Way received their share of my custom that day. It occurred to me, as I downed yet another tall glassful, that pilgrims might pay homage to St James, but more truly their devotion turned towards San Miguel.

Whatever the patron saint, this was another country, with its own language, food, and architecture, with small hidden fields and rich pasture, quite reminiscent of the west of Ireland, and a distinctive music played upon a variant of the bagpipes. As so often, the graffiti pointed the way, and many signposts had been insistently corrected by hand, the Spanish "J" replaced by "X" (Xunta instead of Junta, for instance: a soft sound, rather like the *ch* in *loch*).

Gallego is recognized as a distinct language, most closely related to Portuguese, but with a number of words of Celtic or Germanic origin. About three million speak it, and it supports its own thriving literature and music. General Franco outlawed it in schools to strengthen national identity and discourage segregation, though he himself was from Galicia and spoke Gallego fluently. With the return of democratic rule the Galicians have embraced their ancestral tongue tightly, and do not look kindly on the Generalissimo.

There is a fierce sense of local identity: unlike most of the rest of the Iberian peninsula, Galicia was never occupied by the Moors; its inhabitants fought off Moorish forces when they attacked Santiago de Compostela. Galicians claim to be of Celtic origin: "Galicia" comes from the same linguistic root as "Gaelic" and "Gaul", and there is evidence that Britons fleeing from Saxon invasion settled in Armorica (modern Brittany) and Gallaecia (modern Galicia) between the fourth and seventh centuries. However, Gallego is a Romance language, a descendant of Latin rather than any variant of the Gaelic/Welsh language group.

My tramp through Galicia gave me no more than the lightest brush with language and culture, but there was no mistaking that we were no longer in Kansas. Quite apart from the vertical landscape, every other house seemed to boast a *horreo* or grain store in its garden. These are essentially elevated roofed boxes of wooden slats, or of brick with aeration holes, or (rather impressively) of granite slabs with narrow gaps between. Ranging from 1 to 10 metres in length, these boxes are set on brick or granite pillars, with overhangs to discourage rodents, and traditionally were used to dry and preserve sweetcorn (or any other crop) in the damp climate. No longer greatly used, with changing agricultural practice, they remain an unofficial symbol of the region. I passed a number recently renovated: clearly a matter of local pride. Many boast crosses at either gable.

The ubiquitous cabbage trees form another distinctive feature. A staple of the Galician diet, with a long thick stalk and a single crown often 8 or 10 feet off the ground, they taste, well, like cabbage.

With a sense of triumph I finally slogged my way up into O'Cebreiro, tugged my forelock briefly to Don Elías, and in the waning light found my way to Albergue Do Cebreiro, a municipal hostel run by the regional government, the Xunta de Galicia. This was an uninspiring modern affair, and had I not been so weary I would have looked for something better. As it was I took advantage of a relatively early arrival to share the inadequate washing and drying machines with a South Korean and a Japanese violinist, communicating mostly in sign language since we had no tongue in common. I bagged a bunk in the crowded dormitory, hung up my poor hat – my poor *rusting* hat, since the wire in the brim was yielding up the ghost – and wandered back into the wet but absurdly picturesque village in search of nutrients.

Despite my earlier high spirits I was out of sorts. My fur, I realized, was not only wet but had been brushed the wrong way. For a start it seemed unfair that the place should be so crowded. Having strained every sinew to reach the spot, it galled me to have to step out of the way for tourist coaches. In addition, I was getting slightly worried: Jan's hips had been troubling her, and Goldhara was still suffering from shin splints. The day's climb had been severe, and it was with considerable relief that I saw the pair of them emerge from the swirling mist. Very tough ladies, these two, and I quickly muted my insulting expressions of concern.

We repaired without delay to a fine local restaurant, to sample the thick local soup (potatoes and tree cabbage) and enjoy the warmth of a massive log fire. The only downside of the evening was the rising wind, which caused a sharp backdraft every time the inn's single door opened, with the result that diners and food alike quickly grew speckled with soot. Jim had joined us by this point, and the two of us discovered a sweet, potent green local liquor called *herbeiro*, which would round off every meal we ate thereafter.

That night confirmed that the bright orange rain hood covering my pack was not up to the job. My sleeping bag was damp, and only the fact that I had stored my garments in plastic bags gave me dry clothing for the following day. My boots were soaked through: the *albergue* did not supply surplus newspaper, as subsequent and better-equipped *albergues* would do, so the next morning (after I had retrieved my entirely distinctive blue/black cagoule from the back of an inattentive and embarrassed Asian girl who was on her way out of the door), I shoved my way into damp footwear before wringing out my long-suffering hat and setting off into the soggy dawn.

I had come to identify with my hat. Resilient and jaunty, it spoke of new horizons and durability. When I grew up, I decided, I wanted to be like my hat.

If O'Cebreiro was up, Triacastela was down.

So said the map, but the day's walked experience added some important nuances in the form of the Alto San Roque and, shortly thereafter, the Alto do Poio (or "Poyo", as the café's stamp prefers). The scramble up to the peak of the second Alto stands in my memory as one of the trickiest and most abrupt of the entire Camino, accomplished with much lurching and grasping of tree roots and plunging through deep, muddy rivulets. The little café at its peak was a welcome respite, full of steam and breakfasting pilgrims. As I emerged from its doorway a couple of croissants later, the wind and rain buffeted the little building and accompanied me insistently on the long path down, with every step capable of turning an ankle.

The Camino teaches you about rain. You can curse it, or you can swim in it. The previous night I had read the following from *The Wilderness Within You*:

> Half way up the hill, the downpour starts. Before five minutes have passed, rain is splashing and gurgling, streams are forming in the gutters, my glasses are all steamed up, my hair is plastered to my head, rain is even dripping down my neck, I am freezing and shivering.

Nothing for it but to pull my coat a bit tighter and keep plodding. I hate the cold. I hate the rain. I hate the wind.

I feel Jesus tap my arm, and squint sideways at him through the downpour. He's grinning at me (why?), his hair stuck to his face in wet rivulets, rain on his eyelashes, his face one whole river of rain.

And he's holding out his hand to me, the rain running over it and dripping up his sleeve.

I take his hand.

The difference comes as shock – like a real shock I mean, like an electric shock. Something powerful. For one thing, it's as though joy courses into my body, my whole being, flowing in until I am saturated with this effervescent joy that fills me until I feel like it could spout out of the top of my head like a whale blowing.

Without my noticing it, my whole body has relaxed. He is walking slowly, and because we're holding hands I have to go slower too, and I can't grip on to my coat either. I have to do what he's doing – walking through rain as if it was sunshine, slowly and joyfully, letting it be cold, letting it be wet. He is holding my hand – what does it matter if it's raining?

There are all kinds of storms that have hit and shaken me, walking through my own particular stretches of wilderness. I'm trying to learn the trick of not hunching my shoulders, not hurrying through to get out of it as fast as I can. If I stop and think about it, I can remember the feeling of his hand in mine, and then here it comes again – he walks with me through the storm, his hand holding mine, and the joy coursing through. All the way home.[87]

---

87 Wilcock, *op. cit.*

I relaxed into the rain. It wasn't going away, and neither was I.

The scenery remained spectacular, such as was visible, but for the next few hours my eyes were firmly fixed on the next boulder. While my legs were still hardening, the walking poles had proved heaven-sent, but now, as I grew stronger, I found myself using them less and less; they were starting to prove an encumbrance even on the tricky descents where my rubber-limbed earlier self had appreciated their aid.

On the way down through the small village of Biduedo I rounded a corner and came upon a fat man riding a small donkey up the steep stone slope, a scene straight out of Central Casting. I turned and looked after the retreating pair with concern. Tim Moore, whose *Spanish Steps* had proved such excellent recreational reading, suggests that no donkey should carry a man. No one had told this poor stolid beast.

At last the ground levelled out, and shortly thereafter I reached that day's destination, Triacastela. The name refers to the three castles that once stood in the vicinity. Nothing remains of these fortresses, and the village's greater importance is that it signals the end of the mountains. There would be hills aplenty ahead, but nothing more. Triacastela was an important stop for pilgrims coming down off the heights, with several hospices, doubtless necessary after the vicissitudes of the previous few days, and an extensive monastery which features in the *Codex Calixtinus*. Nearby lie the limestone quarries that provided the materials for the construction of Santiago Cathedral. It became a matter of honour and devotion for medieval pilgrims to carry a block of stone from here for the remaining 150 kilometres. Good grief.

In the Complexo Xacabeo, the warm, pleasant hostel where that evening I hung my hat and dried my socks, I met a couple of ladies from Colorado and South Dakota whose primary concern was the lack of wildlife. Both lived in relatively suburban areas, but both were all too familiar with the regular appearance of herds of deer in their gardens, to the point where any conventional form of horticulture was ruled out. "The only time they disappear," said one, "is when there's a mountain lion around."

Where in Spain, they wanted to know, were the birds?

I had already noticed this on the barren Meseta. But even wild Galicia seemed devoid of creatures, possibly because it was the hunting season. I walked through a land where little stirred. I had seen a couple of snakes, crushed on the road, and in Galicia I came across the small, sad, squished corpses of salamanders, too sluggish in the falling temperatures to cross with despatch. Outside Astorga I had watched some splendid black squirrels at play. In a Galician stream I had the pleasure of seeing a busy little dipper, a bird I had only read about, bobbing up and diving again in the strong current. And of course there had been the vultures in the Pyrenees, the proto-eagles in Belorado, and the unseen storks had left their nests.

It seemed a small haul, however, for weeks of walking. In the heights of the Galician mountains packs of Iberian wolves roam, and a few European brown bears, but this I knew only from wayside noticeboards. Generally the land was silent, devoid of birdsong, free of butterflies, bare of beetles. But perhaps I was simply blind: what did the salamanders eat?[88]

The creatures of Spain may have been notable by their absence, but at least in partial compensation the days in Galicia offered a handsome alternative: utterly enormous sweet chestnuts, hundreds of years old, vast of bole, cragged and weathered and contorted by the seasons, but still heavy with fruit. I delighted in these monsters, surely ancient when Darwin was a boy, and lost no opportunity to stand and rest my hand on them in homage, partaking of their strength.

---

88 Spiders, slugs, worms, and other invertebrates, since you ask. Salamanders are not black and yellow lizards, but amphibians, and are both beautiful and remarkable, capable of regrowing tails and legs in a matter of days. Some species are entirely aquatic. That day I counted five small corpses on the rarely travelled roads, so they are relatively common in this damp corner of Iberia.

Sarria – Portomarín
Days 28 and 29

*I*t was now less than 140 kilometres to Santiago, or about 83 miles. As the end point approached, the steady stream of pilgrims started to increase; from Sarria onwards the influx would grow more notable, as Sarria with its railway station is a convenient starting place for those who wish to qualify for a *compostela*, a certificate of pilgrimage, but lack time or inclination to undertake the whole. (You need to have walked at least 100 kilometres to qualify.) Brierley, entirely fairly, warns long-distance pilgrims not to condescend or criticize. Ahem, wouldn't dream of it, cough.

The day started before dawn, as usual. After a leisurely start and a lingering coffee I was on the road soon after eight with a sharp climb up through sweet chestnut woodland to the Alto do Riocabo. There followed a pleasant stroll in the country as the rain eased off, agreeable but unexceptional. Many long passages of this kind exist on the Camino, neither arduous nor remarkable, gentle to the feet and the spirit.

As the day brightened the sunlight fell on the astonishing volume of fruit scattering the road, not only sweet chestnuts but apples, pears, grapes, walnuts, figs: a land of bounty, only wanting hands to collect it. As I walked I munched. In a wayside bar I met a Korean couple who had amassed a haul of chestnuts, ready for the evening meal, and we fell into conversation. The husband, whose English was impressive, told me that in Korea fishermen will sally forth with the necessary accoutrements to turn their catch into instant sashimi, thinly sliced and consumed with wasabi and soy sauce. In my angling youth I had sampled on occasion bread paste and even ground bait, my mother's lunchtime sandwiches proving insufficient, but this was al fresco dining of another order, and I vowed henceforth to look upon roach and perch with a more seeing eye.

I made it to Sarria by one, and there in a bar I came across Roger, the English building consultant turned cabinet maker, who with a little encouragement was only too pleased to give me names of magazines, books, artisans, colleges. A productive meeting in a productive land.

I found a place to lay my head at the Albergue Don Alvaro, which I chose because it offered a pilgrims' reading room, no less. On exploration this proved to contain a selection of dodgy Italian magazines, but the young bearded owner of the private hostel was kind and helpful, there was a pleasant garden with a fishpond and small daughter cycling around, and in the weak autumn sunshine I sat and savoured the last few chapters of Tim Moore's book. Tim had proved a genial and informative companion. He makes the point that the Camino teaches the value of simple pleasures – a kind welcome, a hot shower, a familiar face in a bar, clean, dry clothes. And a bottom bunk, I added mentally. In fact this *albergue* was above the common run: it boasted a recreation room with a log fire, and I came back from supper to find a multilingual conversation and a bottle of *herbeiro* being passed from hand to hand.

In the steep little street through the old quarter of Sarria I encountered Goldhara, and that night at table we were joined by a talkative lady, whom I will call Nancy, from New York. She was an interesting person, full of zest, with a regularly updated bucket list, but her thousand-watt personality grated.

On a couple of occasions I have undertaken a Myers-Briggs test and established that in terms of I and E, Introvert and Extrovert, I am balanced at the halfway point: my batteries are recharged by both company and solitude. The Camino offered both, in generous measure. But that night I didn't linger over coffee.

The following day offered a steep climb over the Alto Páramo to Portomarín. Whatever Jesus might have to say about the delights of walking in the rain, within an hour I was drenched to the bone. The road led through a string of tiny, slate-roofed hamlets, wet and green, redolent with liquid cow dung and loud with the bellowing of beasts, easily audible above the roar of the downpour. At one point I took shelter in a barn entrance with a barrel-chested, dripping young Spaniard, a pair of townies entirely out of place in this deeply rural economy. Here, as we gradually neared Santiago, the sense of emptiness receded: the farmers we saw were for the most part rich in years, but these were living communities.

Despite the rain it was a genial morning, the woods around me echoing to "All around my hat". I strode along thinking of all that an HND in cabinet-making might involve, and what other delights might come my way. A major birthday was just over the horizon: what lay ahead?

You approach Portomarín by the long road bridge over the Belesar reservoir, created in 1962 when the valley of the Río Miño was flooded. As I ambled down the forest track towards the bridge, my toe caught in a stone and I fell headlong, barely able to twist so that my rucksack took some of the impact.

I lay winded for a couple of moments, trapped beneath the pack.

Help arrived in the form of a young Australian girl, providentially a nurse, who had been walking some distance behind me and panted up, clearly expecting to find a heart attack on her hands. With her assistance I freed myself and was able to scramble to my feet, feeling a dolt but not obviously damaged. I had been extremely lucky, but was badly shaken. When, after a few moments sitting beside the road, I told my rescuer – Carly – that I was fit to continue, she looked at me quizzically. She helped me clamber to my feet and hovered protectively.

It was the only accident of my Camino. I had predicted at the outset that I might fall off something. It could have been a lot worse.

The subsequent walk across the road bridge into Portomarín, however, took all my courage. The bridge stands high above the reservoir, and heights bother me; the wind was strong; huge lorries thundered past continuously, mere inches from the walkway. About halfway across I found myself afflicted with an attack of the shakes, and gave myself a mental pep talk before continuing, one hand clasped to my head to keep my hat from flying free towards the reservoir below.

The walkway ends in a long flight of stairs up into the little town, and the physical challenge helped to steady my nerves. At the top I thanked Carly for her care and stumbled off into the steep cobbled streets, empty at siesta time.

More or less at random I found myself a billet at the Albergue Ultreia. "Ultreia" is a common greeting on the Camino, and derives from the Galician equivalent to the Latin "ultra". It means, variously, "Onward!" "Walk on!" "Pick your feet up, you pitiful streak of grease!" The *albergue* was clean, and the proprietor kindly directed me to a clothes dryer. I showered and changed, then – still trembling – found an open bar to serve me a *bocadillo*. What a wuss.

I sat and thought. The accident could have been so much worse: a knee, a hip. My family does not make old bones, actuarially speaking. What truly mattered?

I limped back up to the *albergue* and sat before the window, staring out at the sheets of rain, and reviewed my options.

> An aged man is but a paltry thing,
> A tattered coat upon a stick...[89]

After my looming retirement, should I train as a guide and offer tours of historic Hastings? Do another degree? Start a literary agency? Make bespoke furniture, should I prove capable? Complete that half-finished novel? Break out my rusty golf clubs, or ask the spiders to return my fishing rods? Like the elves, sink gracefully into the west?

I shook myself. One tumble, and you go all philosophical.

---

89 W. B. Yeats, "Sailing to Byzantium"

Portomarín was moved in the 1960s to accommodate rising water levels, an event commemorated in the town's bars, several of which showed images of the old village, still visible today when the water is low.

One of its most striking features is the Church of San Xoán, a twelfth-century Romanesque fortress-church constructed by the Order of St John of Jerusalem. When the reservoir was planned the entire building was moved, stone by stone, up the steep valley sides to its new location, and fifty years on the numbering on the blocks is still clearly visible. It's a grim, dark edifice, brooding and severe. Although I am not particularly psychic I found it a struggle to walk around.

The Camino reinforced for me that particular places have spiritual power. *Duh*, you may respond, and you would be right, but I tend to choose the fast lane, and have drunk deeply of the waters of materialism. It was not until I joined a church in Hastings with a particularly strong sense of the holy that I started to grow alert to the resonances of place. So, when I walked around the bleak exterior of San Xoán and my spirit flinched, I thought: there is something amiss. Was I sensing its Crusader past?

On the other hand, storks nest on its twin towers.

In the town square I found Goldhara, Jan, and Hume, and together we repaired to a local pizzeria. Nancy again joined our table, a lady lacking volume control, and after our meal Hume and I walked away with a sense of relief.

Later that night I learnt, with shame at my haste to judge, that she had bought dog food for a pitiable stray we met in the square, and had sat on the flagstones to feed him.

Palas de Rei – Ribadiso
Days 30 and 31

After my fall I could not find a comfortable position for my battered earth suit, and slept badly.

But the following day was a gentle amble, in better weather, through groves of chestnut and eucalyptus, crossing a series of river valleys and heading generally downhill.

I knew they were an alien invader, destined for the pulp industry, but I loved the eucalyptus forests. I find the trees wonderfully elegant and fragrant, and to walk among them for hours at a time was heavenly. From an ecological point of view they are disastrous, as they have drastically replaced the native forest cover and sustain little wildlife, but my fickle soul rejoiced.

This locality has a turbulent past. An hour or so after leaving Portomarín, the Way passes through the little village of Castromaior, the name referring to the large hill fort (*castro*) whose remains are still visible on the rising ground to the west. The foundations of a Roman camp have also been discovered on the outskirts. Shortly thereafter you enter Hospital, site of a pilgrim infirmary, long vanished, and then the village of Ventas de Narón. This hamlet also boasted a pilgrim hospital, built by the Knights Templar in the thirteenth century. More significantly, in the year 820, a few years after the discovery of the tomb of St James, the Christians gained a bloody victory over the troops of the Emir of Córdoba here. So recorded the historians of Christendom, but it was probably no more than one of hundreds of skirmishes as successive Emirs consolidated their grip – by 929 the Emirate covered most of the Iberian peninsula, and a later Emir proclaimed himself a Caliph, emphasizing his independence from Damascus and competing with Tunis for control of North Africa. Islamic rule in Iberia did not end until 1492, with the expulsion of the Moors (a loose term) from Granada.

A few kilometres further on lies the ancient hamlet of Ligonde, now a tiny settlement but once a significant stopping point; Charlemagne reputedly stayed here, and centuries later it hosted a *Cementerio de Peregrinos*.

The day's destination was Palas de Rei, the Palace of the King. But what palace, and which king? Archaeological remains and dolmens are common in the area, and it seems possible that the monarch in question was the Visigoth king Wittiza, who reigned between AD 702 and 710. King Wittiza was notable for his efforts to stem corruption in the Catholic Church, and for reversing some of the harsher edicts of his hated but formidable father Ergica. The settlement antedates the Camino, and appears in Aymeric Picaud's guide.

I found this history fascinating. The entire Camino Frances seems to be woven about political and racial fault lines. Here was a clear example, the Way in the space of a single day crossing the shifting boundary between Moorish and Christian Iberia.

Hume and I spent much of the day walking together, talking priestcraft. Sermon preparation; the healing ministry; the place of liturgy; pastoral care; church politics and how to get round the choirmaster, on which Hume was loquacious; the importance of mission, on which he was not. I tentatively broached the issue of the spiritual disciplines, but this was a door locked tight, and I did not insist.

That night we found our way to a modest hostel, the Albergue Buen Camino, with solid wooden bunks under a vaulted wooden ceiling, and good facilities. To no one's surprise we met Goldhara and Jan, and with them wandered off in search of a good *pulperia*.[90] We were joined by two newcomers to our little group, Jackie and Shirley Ann, a couple of Canadians.

Why should Galicia, one of the more mountainous quarters of Spain, have developed such a gastronomic speciality as octopus braised with paprika and served smoking hot on a wooden platter? By this point in the journey every pint-sized township boasted such a restaurant, often offering an accompanying delicacy of small green roasted *padrone* peppers doused in olive oil and dusted with sea salt.

For those who find the idea revolting, set your prejudices to one side. I assure you this is not a gastronomic experience

---

90   Originally, a rural grocery store and drinking establishment, but in this context meaning "octopus restaurant".

to miss. I first came across octopus in the Greek islands, where the day's catch is commonly suspended from the rails supporting the café awnings, causing a shock to unwary customers and amusement to the rest of us.

You could see why octopus would feature on a menu in Skiathos or Kos. But why inland Galicia?

In a moment of wickedness – I was dining with five North Americans – I explained that octopi took advantage of the high local rainfall to make their way up the mountain streams to breed.[91] There were expressions of interest and nodding heads around the table, and I let the matter rest. For the next couple of nights I listened to Goldhara and Jan explaining this piece of newfound knowledge to other pilgrims before I finally fessed up. It is entirely possible that this item of folklore is being passed from pilgrim to pilgrim even now.

British humour, whimsical and sly, is often incomprehensible to our American cousins. My stepdaughter Grace, who is married to an American, suggests that the cultural melting-pot of the States has required the development of jokes more clearly signalled, less obliquely inserted into conversation.

The cultural difference is particularly in evidence if you compare British television adverts with their American counterparts. A British advert for, say, Volkswagen will feature a variety of dogs gazing happily from car windows, the badge barely glimpsed, manufacturer mentioned only in the closing moments. Brits love this understatement. An American equivalent will not only boast about the size,

---

91 I thought about singing them a traditional Galician fisherman's song, but this would have been over the top.

power, shininess, and sex appeal of the car in question, but will handily sideswipe other models or dealerships. Of course this one's better, trust me. No, really, trust me.

Despite my mischief-making the evening ended peacefully, with due appreciation of *herbeiro*. But a piece of news we received had galvanized Hume.

The Cathedral of St James in Santiago has many claims to fame, but one of the most spectacular, the lighting of the thurible (incense burner) or *botafumeiro*, takes place somewhat irregularly. It costs an eye-watering sum to fill and operate it, so unless a special mass has been commissioned by a group willing to stump up the price, it only appears about thirty times a year.

Two days hence, we learned, there would be one such mass, and Hume was not intending to miss it. If he were to rise early and walk late, he reckoned, he could cover three days' journey in two big stages. By the time I woke the following morning he was packed and gone.

The rest of us decided to take our chances in respect of the *botafumeiro*, and in any case another challenge presented itself. Jackie, a slim, dark-haired lady, had been suffering from occasional acute attacks of vertigo. She was travelling with a friend of many years, Shirley Ann, who had been her superior officer in the Canadian Army. However, Shirley Ann's knees had completely rebelled (she was scheduled for urgent surgery on her return to Canada, and was taking a taxi from one hostel to another), so I walked with Jackie for the next couple of days.

Jackie proved genial company, and suffered no further attacks. She was walking the Camino after a distressing divorce a couple of years previously, simply to affirm that she could make it on her own. Her husband, like her a career officer in the Canadian Army, had been traumatized by a stint in Afghanistan, and their marriage had foundered after his return. Jackie was very close to her two sons, both of whom had followed her into the army – her older lad, Sean, now a commissioned officer, is 6'8", and has found himself a girlfriend of 6'2".[92] Both boys, Sean and her younger son Colin, were now serving in the Canadian military, and she was very proud of them.

Jackie told me something about her life: she had served in the military for twenty-two years, much of it as a dental hygienist. Now she enjoyed a portfolio lifestyle, combining work as a hygienist with driving a school bus (the army having taught her how to handle trucks) and occasional service as a prison guard. She also acted as a simplicity advisor, helping women, mainly elderly, to downsize and declutter. A resourceful person and a survivor, she clearly relished this diversity of occupations.

One anecdote from her army days stuck in the mind: she had been teamed with an Inuit recruit for a search and rescue exercise in Canada's endless forests. They were trained, given equipment, and hiked in, but her companion was completely baffled, having never previously seen a tree. Nevertheless, the pair proved adept at map-reading, and won the competition handily.

I treasured such conversations, the chance to savour

---

92 I noted this information out of interest, but really it is of little consequence. I am just over 6 feet; my son-in-law Dan is 6'4". The days when I could loom over a room are long past. Today's youngsters can pat me on the head, and my grandchildren will shake their heads at pictures of their dwarfish granddad.

another person's story. The world of work is curiously isolating, the constant deadlines leaching away the chance to chat, and the Camino afforded time.

The route that day took us across a series of shallow watersheds – eight streams or rivers in the course of 16 miles. Just outside Palas de Rei we passed *Campos dos Romeiros*, the field of the pilgrims, where in past times travellers gathered, assembling in a band to journey together for safety.

Signs were starting to mention Santiago. For several days we had been passing kilometre stones ticking down the distance, though Jackie refused to look as she found the slow decrease a strain on her spirits. Canadians measure in kilometres, I discovered: how had I not known this? To me the waystones seemed to arrive wonderfully swiftly, but I was aware of the impending end, and keen to taste every moment.

Around midday we reached Melide, which boasts itself the *pulpo* (octopus) capital of the world, and there we waved to Goldhara, Jan, and Jim, who were testing the claim. We pressed on, despite the increasing precipitation.

Conversation was intermittent, as right through from departure to arrival the rain bucketed down, hour after hour, the wettest day of the entire journey. I had my clothes wrapped in plastic, and my rucksack had its cover, but nothing could ward off the downpour. By the time we arrived in the tiny hamlet of Ribadiso that night and hooked up with Shirley Ann, both bedding and boots were sopping. So were my passport and money, and I spread my precious paperwork out on my bunk to dry. Happily Albergue Los Caminantes provided not only efficient dryers, but newspapers to stuff in our boots: clearly they expected to shelter soggy pilgrims. My cagoule and hat I hung over a chair to drip. Shirley Ann gave me a vast plastic sack to cover my pack. My copy of Brierley (soaking, frayed, and very dog-eared – could a guidebook publisher ask for more?) I left for a needy traveller, Jackie having passed to me a pristine copy she found abandoned in an *albergue* a day or two back.

The trek had taken its toll, and by nine all lights were out.

O Pedrouzo – Santiago
Day 32

The following morning dawned grey and chilly. The threatened rain held off, and the day's stroll through eucalyptus plantations was agreeable, but not worth a paragraph of your time. We made it to O Pedrouzo, an undistinguished little settlement, by 2.00, where we found Shirley Ann waiting for us. Having located an adequate but unexceptional *albergue*, I wandered off in search of a late lunch.

Just as I was finishing a plate of roasted peppers my mobile rang: Pen! In the deserted café I sat and chatted with her for ages. Her main news was that she had scheduled a trip to the States – her first – to see some online friends and visit one of the oldest Quaker meeting houses in New England, where a friend was giving a lecture. It was an expensive journey for just a few days, but it felt absolutely right, and my intrepid wife was not in the least fazed by the challenge of finding her way across New York and taking a train to Boston.

Jan and Goldhara had found a far nicer hostel down the road, happily, because Jan's hip completely gave up halfway through the day and her big sister insisted they take a cab. The poor woman was in a lot of pain, but determined to complete the journey. We had one day to go.

Goldhara offered news of Hume: he had covered 47 kilometres the previous day, despite the blinding rain, and was on track to see his *botafumeiro*. She and he had agreed a rendezvous for the following evening, at the cathedral.

Jackie and Shirley Ann, Goldhara, Jan, and I met that night for another taste of *pulpo*, but we were all feeling the oppression that comes with impending departure. I went back to the hostel, and sat in the mud-coloured little lounge beneath a muted television. It had been a long adventure, and a rich one. What awaited?

The following day I left my walking poles in the rack for anyone who might want them. They had played their part. It felt like a graduation.

That final morning I was up well before dawn to walk to Santiago with Goldhara. Jan was completing her pilgrimage by cab; Shirley Ann was planning to walk the final stage, come what may, so I relinquished her and Jackie into one another's care.

By this point Goldhara and I had heard many of each other's stories, so we walked in silence, willing to appreciate together this last day on the road.

After an hour we came to a little roadside café, hosted by a woman who had spent thirty years in Britain, married to a guy from Sussex, running a similar establishment. With his death she had returned to her native Galicia, and had found a ready market for a full English: bacon and eggs, baked beans and tomatoes, mushrooms and fried bread, served with English mustard and brown sauce. This was coronary fare of the very finest, and we fell upon our platefuls with glee. The proprietor sat and chatted with us, glad to talk of people and places she had known across the Channel.

As we were finishing Jan turned up, having determined to try to make the last day on foot after all: she was nearly in tears, however, and we sat with her until a cab arrived.

When we set off again Goldhara told me of a trip she and two girlfriends had made about twenty years previously. A friend had flown them to a lake in Alaska, landing by seaplane, and they agreed that he would pick them up from another lake, in a different catchment, a couple of weeks later. They chose not to hunt or fish, so their food and camping gear for the fortnight had to be carried with them.

All went well for several days, until one afternoon as they made camp they spotted a grizzly bear a mile or so away on the shore of a lake, trotting steadily in their direction. Nothing they could do would cause the animal to turn aside, they had no weapons, and they became increasingly frightened as the massive and very dangerous creature lumbered their way. Then Goldhara had remembered something she had been told: an American Indian belief that bears would not attack women.

Together she and one of her companions dropped the saucepans they had been banging and lifted their tops. The bear immediately changed course, ambled past their camp, and disappeared over the brow of the hill. He had come within 20 yards.

I asked if Goldhara was still in touch with her friends. Yes, with one of them, she responded. The other had been so utterly scared that for the rest of the fortnight she withdrew totally into herself, completely silent, and had remained estranged ever since.

And so we walked into Santiago, thirty-two days after I had set out.

As we neared the outskirts, we caught up with Pierre and Brigitte. It was lovely to see them again. I made the introductions and spent a happy hour acting as translator: we were all infected with the sense of culmination, and laughed and clowned for the last hour into town.

In the centre of the city we went our separate ways. Goldhara needed to seek out somewhere without too many stairs, for Jan's benefit, while Pierre and Brigitte had arranged to meet friends.

I opted to stay at the Seminario Menor La Asunción, stern and stark, filled with dormitories: just the kind of forbidding environment for knocking young students into shape. For all I knew such accommodation might be far preferable to the poor students' home environments, but somehow I doubted it. Shades of Colditz. There were small cubicles on the top floor (probably servants' quarters) and I booked my first private room in a month. I dropped my bag on the floor and looked around: privacy. My own space. How alien. I showered, then found my way down, and down, and up and up, into the old town and the cathedral where I would obtain my *compostela*.

The Dean's office in the precincts of the Cathedral of St James was crowded with chattering pilgrims shouting greetings and telling stories. One by one the queue crept forward. Behind a long desk a series of administrators bent over their task, each asking your name and your reason for undertaking your pilgrimage. The *compostela* is in Latin, and the Latinized form of your name – in the accusative case, so mine reads *Anthonium Petrum Collins* – is inscribed in the appropriate spot.

I emerged into the weak autumn sun clutching my tube of cardboard. Outside the cathedral I ran into Jan, Goldhara, Jim, Hume, Jackie, Shirley Ann, and several other folk, including Carrine, the Swiss girl, and Jean Michel, a young man with French and American parents, still closely wrapped around the lass he had met en route, the couple whom I had last seen waiting for Compline in Léon.

Dizzy with delight and achievement, we sat in the sunshine outside a café and beamed at one another, sinking glass after glass of tart white wine, engaging in cross-currents of "do you remember?" and generally celebrating, gleeful we had made it through.

Hume had reached the city in time, and seen his *botafumeiro* (he was still glowing and voluble from the experience). We toasted him, and one another, the spirit of fiesta strong upon us. It was the end of term; we had been let out of class; the results were in, and we had all passed.

I texted Pen, Carrie, and Abbie.

Minutes later Pen rang, to say a monster storm was heading for Britain and could I delay my flight? Alarming headlines about impending doom filled the British press, and her concern was well placed: the "St Jude's Storm" or "Cyclone Christian" would leave 600,000 homes without power in Britain and kill people across Europe.

Jolted, I left my friends to return to the Seminario, to see what was possible.

No human being at Ryanair proved accessible by computer, so, reflecting that the company would not fly if it were not safe, I decided to check in online.

I was unable, however, to find a working printer at the hostel, to print out my boarding pass, and with a certain degree of panic made my way back, late in the afternoon (down and down, and up and up), to the pilgrimage resource centre, which for two euros was willing to find my reference with Ryanair and to print out the necessary document. Several hours of intense frustration, crowned with success: I could have kissed the helpful girl at the centre, who was clearly well used to dealing with frantic pilgrims.

I had missed a rendezvous with the Wine Sisters, so enjoyed a solitary late pizza before wandering back, down and up, to the Seminario. I spotted a figure ahead of me, somewhat bowed but coping easily with the steep slope, and as I drew level – that competitive edge not completely dulled – I realized I was walking with Cristiane, the elderly French woman whose kindness I had so appreciated in Burgos. She had just completed the Camino Primitivo: a very tough route, and a very tough old lady. One of the unanticipated blessings of the Camino is its abundance of such women.

The following morning I set out to explore Santiago, but found the city centre empty. Granted it was a Sunday, but even so I wandered the old stone streets and the shuttered precincts for nearly an hour before I found a bar to sell me a hot chocolate and croissant, both utterly delicious.

Finally, a waiter told me what a more diligent pilgrim would have known: the clocks had gone back that night. Feeling a clot, I headed for the cathedral, climbing the long steps and passing under the towering stone façade to the feast of gold and wood, statuary and incense within. I paused for a moment at the entrance to breathe the heavenly aroma: Christianity at its most sensual.

Under the main altar lies a crypt, deserted at that early hour. You can descend the steps to pray at the tomb of St James, whose immaculate marble sarcophagus is on display. I stared at it, the petty thought coming to my mind that this was probably not the same sarcophagus that had ferried the saint across the Mediterranean, through the Straits of Gibraltar, and up the Spanish coast.

By nature I am sceptical, critical, dubious. A question mark is engraved on my breastplate. Count me among the mockers.

But, alone in the low-ceilinged vault, and against my will, I had no choice. There was, quite abruptly, a pervading Presence, gentle but inexorable. I sank to my knees and prayed, for St James might not have been there, but the Holy Spirit was.

Men have attached the name of God to all kinds of experiences, so I simply record what happened. When I pray, I occasionally feel a gentle Presence standing just behind my shoulder. When I pray with others, the whole can seem much greater than the sum of the parts. When I speak in tongues, an exaltation, a coherent sense of blessing, may come upon me.

This was different: somewhere between an orgasm and a sneeze, an abrupt shock, a jolt from many years ago, so unanticipated that I felt dislocated.

It felt as if I had been mugged by the Almighty, who had seen the flimsiness of my reservations, and swept them aside.

Decades previously I had joined a slow queue at Taizé to pray at an icon of the crucified Christ. Very unsure, as a good evangelical, whether I was doing the right thing, I had crafted a doctrinally accurate prayer that listed my caveats and crossed all the theological Ts. When my turn came I knelt down, cautiously put my forehead to the wood of the icon – and was flooded by the joy and merriment of the Father's love, driving the words of my little construct clear out of my mind.

Now, as I knelt alone before that blocky tomb, it was as if He were looking at me and saying, "What took you so long?"

At 12.00 I made my way back, from a foray for presents, to the cathedral, in good time for the pilgrim mass. The place was already thronged, and became increasingly packed, with hundreds standing. The mass was formulaic, the Spanish homily entirely predictable, as I learned from a neighbour: an opportunity missed – and why, in a building crammed with pilgrims and tourists, was there no concession to the multilingual congregation?

However, at the end of the service the *botafumeiro* was unhitched, filled, lit, and set swinging, eight red-robed burly men on the other end.

The thurible stands 4 feet high, weighing as much as a grown man, and the rope is long. Gradually it picks up speed. As it reaches the zenith of its arc it looks as if the censer will impact the distant ceiling. It is unimaginably exhilarating to see this hunk of metal, trailing smoke and flame, come swooping towards you, mere feet above your head. Look up, Jean-Paul had advised me: could I do anything else?

I was sitting directly in its path, and as it descended upon us a little girl in the row behind me shrieked and shrieked with terror and joy.

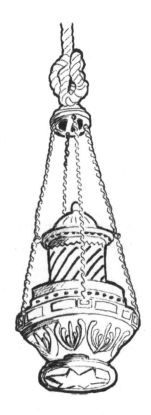

The Naked Pilgrim
Day 33, and counting

Santiago was a culmination.

The following dawn I climbed into my cab and was hustled – the speed making me uneasy, after weeks of plod – across the sleeping town and out to the airport. Before I boarded the plane there was a brief altercation with Ryanair about the size of my pack, which I resolved by forcing it brutally into the metal framework provided as a guide.

A few brief hours later Pen met me at Hastings station. We embraced awkwardly, the weeks of absence between us. As I carried my rucksack through the front door our cats fled: nothing new there. After a brief session of greetings I set to work to cleanse the grime and odour of the Way from my possessions, stuffing my sleeping bag into the washing machine and sorting socks from sweaters. My pack was swiftly relegated to the shed, and thence to Freecycle.

The mental adjustment took far longer.

Imagine yourself walking down your street. Around you invisible whiskers reach out, tasting the air, reading the adverts, greeting the trees, evaluating other pedestrians for threat or fashion sense or sex appeal. You move through a web of associations, memories, league tables, relationships – past, present, and future swirling and coalescing with every step and thought. Here you bought an ice cream; there you donated some crockery; that carpet shop has a sale on and the front room needs a bigger rug. Number 16 has a new car, a Volvo. You smile at your neighbour, exchange a few genial words, pat their dog, ask after their grandchild. You are home.

Home has layers, an accretion of years of small choices, reciprocal kindnesses, extra miles, shared jokes and irritations and enthusiasms. Home is rich humus. Home is children's drawings and stains on the walls. At home you know where to find the tea caddy.

To be a pilgrim is to step apart. This is not the heady sensation of a holiday, a brief snatch of freedom, a moment of license. It is a new experience, in a minor key, set to an unknown tune. Your home is on your back. So much that is familiar is stripped away. The sense associations and homely smells vanish. A pilgrim lays aside reputation, language, and function.

Every morning brings fresh smells and sights, tastes and accents. You quickly develop routines – wash this, fold that, refill, hide, adjust, check – but there is no security beyond what you carry in your mind or on your back. You ride the wave of novelty.

There are compensations. The first is the Road itself, the ever-magnetic horizon, which provides purpose and goal. The second is the company: pilgrims willingly share interesting stories and attitudes.

A pilgrim quickly learns frugality, to appreciate small details. A ray of sunshine, a weathered stone, a chocolate bar, a sandwich of air-cured ham, a cat on a wall: these are matters to be savoured, the cat an instant friend.

One of the blessings of the Road, should you wish it, is solitude. You grow swiftly aware of the tens of thousands of seekers who have preceded you, but they are silent. The spiritual, so easily relegated to the margins, is there at your elbow. On the Way – at least, on the main pilgrim routes – you know that at day's end you will find a church, a shrine, a place for your spirit to find peace, if peace has eluded you.

Returning, you see things differently. Your old niche no longer fits. Odd details suddenly assume new prominence. A quick stroll to the shops demands your full attention. Back amongst your friends and peers, as amongst your family, conversation suddenly lapses. Easy chatter seems beyond you. Details – sports results, *Strictly*, celebrities, economic and political news – fail to grasp your attention.

I love my job, but it required a real effort of the imagination to think my way back into it, like struggling into a heavy overcoat.

It was easier with family and friends: after the initial flurry had passed, my lovely people scooted sideways, made space, helped me to send out roots again. The intimacy of the ordinary gradually replaced the intimacy of the Way.

Yet something had changed, permanently.

There is a shellfish, a limpet, which lives in the liminal area between low and high tide, suctioned powerfully to its rock to withstand the battering water. It roves locally, but returns to its place with each tide, over the years cutting a groove in the hard stone.

I felt as if I had been, for decades, a human limpet, content to flourish where planted, personally, culturally, theologically, professionally. Two things had jolted me entirely: firstly, my marriage to Pen, a lady for whom no room stays the same two weeks running, and who has taught me the value of non-attachment, so far as clothing, books, and personal clutter are concerned. Now the Road had spoken to me, changing the way I saw myself: I was no longer simply a publisher, a husband, a father, a friend. I had tasted, fleetingly, the edge of something very big. It was only the start of the adventure, but now I was a pilgrim.

Coda

So, O pilgrim, what did you discover? Was the journey worth the candle?

These were some of the things I learned.

- The Road gets under your skin, and into your soul. You are free, you can stop where you will, you may eat what you can find and afford, but no pilgrim stays still for long. The horizon calls.

- You may meet the Almighty, or the Infinite; you will certainly meet yourself. I had not expected my soul to be pinned out for examination like a flayed frog.

- Your conscience will grow more tender.

- Boredom helps this process.

- Moments of holiness may smite you on the forehead, like a rake in the grass. When you least expect it, whup.

- You make splendid friends. My mate Douglas the vicar told me as much, but I had not really anticipated the degree to which the experience creates a bond.

- Once a pilgrim, always a pilgrim. I shall return to the Way.

- Your capacity for solitude will surprise you. So will your capacity for prayer.

- You will grow impatient of lies.

- Your appetite for stuff will diminish.

- You will develop a stronger truth sense.

- You will laugh a lot.

- Your family, and your friends, assume greater importance.

- Your career may not.

- Ask a llama politely for a pair of socks.

You can find me on Facebook.

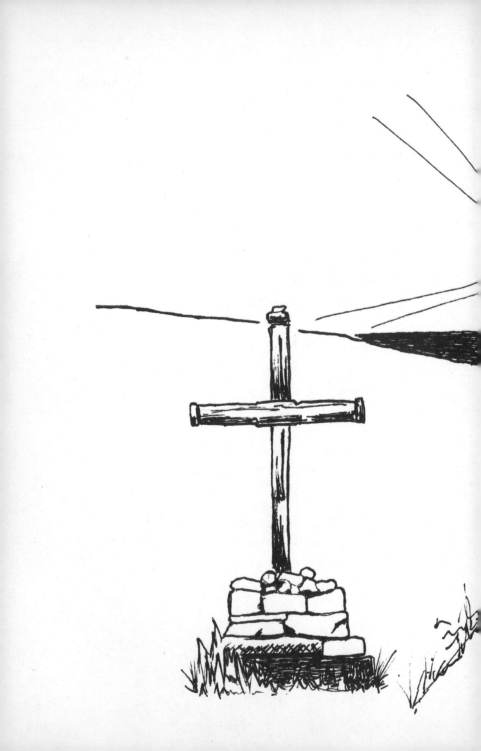

The Prayer of the Pilgrims

Lord, who called your servant Abraham out of the town of Ur in Chaldea, and who watched over him during his wanderings; who guided the Jewish people through the desert: we ask you to watch over your present servants, who for love of your name make a pilgrimage to Santiago de Compostela.

Be for us
A companion on our journey
Our guide at crossroads
Our strength when we grow weary
Our fortress in danger
Our resource in our wanderings
Our shade in the day's heat
The light in our darkness
A consolation when we are low in spirits

And the power behind our intention
So that we, under your guidance, safely and unhurt, may
reach the end of our journey, and strengthened with
gratitude and power, secure and filled with happiness,
may find our way home.
Through Jesus Christ our Lord,
Amen

Select Bibliography

Brierley, John, *A Pilgrim's Guide to the Camino de Santiago*, Camino Guides, an imprint of Findhorn Press, 9th edition, 2013. Highly recommended if you are planning to walk the Camino Francés.

Holland, Tom, *Millennium*, Abacus, an imprint of Little, Brown, 2008. Colourful and packed with delicious nuggets.

Moore, Tim, *Spanish Steps: Travels with My Donkey*, Vintage, 2005. A very readable account of walking the Camino Francés with the additional burden of a four-legged beast.

Rufin, Jean-Christoph, *Immortelle randonée: Compostelle malgré moi*, Editions Guérin, 2013. A personal and entertaining account of walking the Camino del Norte, the northern route.

Sumption, Jonathan, *Pilgrimage*, Faber and Faber, 1975. Sumption brings an informative but sceptical eye to bear on the whole phenomenon of pilgrimage.